How thinking about God shapes
Australia

Theology Matters

Peter Sherlock & Daniel Nellor

Published in Australia by
Coventry Press
33 Scoresby Road
Bayswater VIC 3153

ISBN 9781922589453

Copyright © Peter Sherlock and Daniel Nellor 2024

All rights reserved. Other than for the purposes and subject to the conditions prescribed under the *Copyright Act*, no part of this publication may be reproduced, stored in a retrieval system, or transmitted in any form or by any means, electronic, mechanical, photocopying, recording or otherwise, without the prior permission of the publisher.

Catalogue-in-Publication entry is available from the National Library of Australia
http://catalogue.nla.gov.au

Cover Image: Libby Byrne, (2022). *Sanctuary III*, 120 x 90 cm, Mixed media on canvas, Melbourne.
Cover design by Ian James – www.jgd.com.au
Text design by Coventry Press
Set in EB Garamond

Printed in Australia

To the staff, students and graduates of the University of Divinity

Shine like stars in the sky

Contents

Foreword	vii
Introduction	1
Frank Brennan	4
Libby Byrne	14
Dan Fleming	22
Anne Pattel-Gray	34
Tony Rinaudo	43
Sean Lau	52
Julie Edwards	61
Stan Grant	70
Rufus Black	80
Deborah Barker	91
Kevin Rudd	99
Conclusion	110
Acknowledgments	116

Foreword

When I was a child, I became aware that the stories of Jesus meant something to me. As I thought about Jesus meeting people in their moments of deepest need, and giving them a future that was incredibly different to the one they had, these stories of God's welcoming love found a home in me and changed my life.

This is theology at work. Theology happens when we think about the love of God and what it might mean for our lives and our world. And theology is not only for clergy like me. As this book shows, Australians from many different walks of life are shaped by thinking about God and about Jesus as revealing God to us.

As an archbishop, I am very aware that the Christian churches are in a crisis of trust. An enormous amount of hurt and grief has been brought to light over the last decade, as it has become clear in how many ways the churches failed their people. At the same time, the world is in crisis too. We see wars and violence, foreign and domestic; the undermining of democracy; the unprecedented advance of technology and the ongoing challenge of climate change. More than ever, we need new ways of thinking. We need ethics, and we need theology.

Whenever I speak about God, I speak about grace. Grace is God's leaning towards humanity; it is the often unexpected appearance of a love that transforms us, that makes our lives different and, by extension, makes our world different. Theology is reflecting on that grace, trying to understand it better, going deeper in order to experience the transformation of our selves and our world that God's love can bring.

As a Christian in Australia, I think we need to learn new ways to live and tell the story of Jesus — and to tell it against the background of another culture, a culture that has survived more than 40,000 years. Our First Peoples have invited Australians, including the churches, to listen to their stories, join their struggles, and take seriously their experiences of the Creator Spirit.

This book is a contribution to the ongoing effort to join with First Peoples and all peoples to think about how our world might look in the light of the welcoming, inclusive and undying love of God. It is not a book of answers. Often theology is about asking better questions. This is a fascinating glimpse into the lives of eleven people who reflect on what their lives and work might mean in a world that is loved by God.

The Most Reverend Kay Goldsworthy AO DD
Archbishop of Perth

Introduction

PETER SHERLOCK

THOUGH I'M NOT a professional theologian, I have been around theology all my life. You might say I was born into it: my first home was in the theological college where my parents – both theologians and eventually both Anglican priests – were teaching and studying. Later, my first job was in a theological bookshop, and my partner of the past 30 years is an Anglican priest. I have been a follower of Jesus all my life and I still read the Bible and pray every day. As I write, I have just finished a 12-year term as Vice-Chancellor of Australia's first theological university, the University of Divinity.

I'm well aware that many Australians are not as deeply invested in the future of theological education as I am. The dictionary defines theology as the study of God and religious belief; and many would argue that nothing could be less relevant to Australia today. European Christianity has – since Anselm of Canterbury coined the phrase a thousand years ago – described the pursuit of theology as 'faith seeking understanding'. Today, however, large numbers of Australians have no religious belief. Meanwhile churches and other religious institutions are deeply discredited in the wake of the Royal Commission into Institutional Responses to Child Sexual Abuse, or associated with unjust forms of discrimination. Surely, then, theology has little to say to Australia.

This book argues the opposite. My co-author Daniel Nellor and I start from the premise that God – whatever 'God' might mean – is something or someone many Australians seek, albeit in various ways and under various names. There is still room in a secular Australia for spirituality, for mystery, for seeking a deeper understanding of who we are, where we are and why we are here. First Nations people know this well, as do many others who are Muslim, Christian, Jewish, Hindu, Buddhist, of other faith traditions or of none at all. The famously atheist broadcaster Phillip Adams often speaks of his sense of the 'numinous', and in doing so he is not at all far from the kind of thing spoken about by theologians.

So if theology does still have something worth saying, worth hearing, and worth acting upon, what difference does it make? To answer this question, we decided not to look at the history of theological education, the curriculum taught in theological colleges and universities, the impact of theology within the churches, or the economic value of theology – areas already traversed by others. Instead, we decided to ask: what difference has theology made in the lives and careers of Australians who have studied, or engaged deeply with, Christian theology?

The result is this book, containing profiles of 11 Australians. It's probably true that most people studying theology in Australia are doing so in order to become a religious minister or play some other official role in a religious institution. But there are many others who do it for different reasons, and it is these we sought out for this book. So we deliberately chose people whose primary contributions to Australian society have been in fields outside the churches. Each has engaged with varieties of theology in the Christian tradition, reflecting the relative dominance and wealth of Christian theological institutions in this land for the past century or so; we acknowledge the need to explore the stories of other theological traditions in the future.

The participants include an activist and an artist, an ethicist and two First Nations elders, an environmental scientist, a lawyer and a social worker, a journalist, an academic, a school principal and a politician and diplomat. Some are household names, others are less well known. Each participant met with us for an interview of an hour or so and, in the weeks after that conversation, we created a profile of them. Each participant had the opportunity to review and amend the profile, and each approved the final chapter as published in this book.

The conversations were rich and wide-ranging, covering an extraordinary range of topics, people and places reflective of our participants' backgrounds and experiences. Some have intentionally pursued theology, motivated by their faith or seeking answers to a big question. For others the journey has been full of surprises; and theology has led them to unexpected places. What they all have in common is that their study of theology – the wrestling they have done with questions about God and the world and social justice and spirituality – has informed their lives and work.

A surprising aspect of these conversations was the common sense of hope for our future, notwithstanding the confronting challenges or thorny issues that each participant wrestles with in their work and calling. As you read these stories and consider for yourself how it is that theology matters, we hope that you might be encouraged in your own journey – and perhaps a little more curious about engaging with theology.

Frank Brennan

Frank Brennan is a Jesuit priest, based in Queensland. He is a Distinguished Fellow of the PM Glynn Institute at Australian Catholic University, an Adjunct Professor at the Thomas More Law School at ACU and research professor at the Australian Centre for Christianity and Culture. He chaired the National Human Rights Consultation for the Rudd Government, was a member of the Turnbull Government's expert panel which conducted the Religious Freedom Review and a member of the Senior Advisory Group on the Co-Design of an Indigenous Voice set up by the Morrison Government. He was awarded an Officer of the Order of Australia (AO) for services to Aboriginal Australians, and is also a recipient of the Humanitarian Overseas Service Medal for his work in Timor Leste when Director of the local Jesuit Refugee Service. The National Trust has classified him as a Living National Treasure.

WHICH SIDE of the river are you on?

This was the question Frank Brennan posed to a group of Year 12 students at Xavier College one day in the 1980s. He had recently returned from a remote Aboriginal community in Queensland where he had been helping the community to secure land rights from the State Government and better housing from the Commonwealth Government. Now he was back in Melbourne teaching a religion class at one of the schools run by his order – the Society of Jesus, or Jesuits. Frank told the students about a conversation he'd had up north. Sitting on a river bank, an Aboriginal woman had pointed across the water to a large mansion on the other side. 'That's Mr X's weekender,' she said. Mr X was a prominent Victorian businessman at the time. 'He's not here very often, but when he comes, he comes by helicopter. You can see the helipad on the roof. He bought that house for a million dollars.' One million dollars was more than the entire sum the community was seeking to build housing for 50 people.

The Xavier boys weren't particularly moved by the story of the Aboriginal community and the millionaire. 'What's wrong with having a weekender?' they asked. 'Don't his taxes pay for Aboriginal welfare? If Aborigines want housing, why don't they build it for themselves?' Frank says today: 'I tried to give all sorts of flash, legal, Jesuit-type answers. But in the end, I said, I can't answer all your questions. I just have one for you. Which side of the river are you standing on when you ask those questions? Can you see that if you stood on the other side of the river, you would have very different questions to ask?'

Theology is less about giving the right answers than asking the right questions. Frank Brennan is an example of a theologically educated Australian who has tried throughout a long career to bring his Christian worldview up against the pressing questions of the day – whether they be questions about the church, or the state, or both. As a Jesuit priest and lawyer, he has walked the corridors of power as well as the halls of immigration detention centres. He has spoken up for the rights of Indigenous Australians and asylum-seekers in public forums and courtrooms around the country. He has served in roles both within the church and without, and is also a regular media commentator.

Frank's father, Sir Gerard Brennan, a committed Catholic, was a longtime Justice of the High Court of Australia and was Chief Justice of Australia from 1993 to 1995. Frank once reflected that the role of the priest in the public square is to 'explain in terms comprehensible to the contemporary individual the significance of God's love and the life God has intended for human kind'

(Brennan, *Gasson Lectures*, 13). In trying to do this, Frank has been unafraid to mix theology and politics. Frank quotes approvingly his fellow Jesuit, Pope Francis, who has stated emphatically that 'a good Catholic meddles in politics' and that 'politics, according to the Social Doctrine of the Church, is one of the highest forms of charity, because it serves the common good' (Brennan, *Amplifying*, 15). By applying faith to politics, by trying to stand on both sides of the river, Frank Brennan has spent a lifetime in pursuit of this common good.

When we spoke to Frank, he was braving Melbourne's sixth COVID lockdown from his home as Rector of Newman College at the University of Melbourne. We asked him to tell us a little about his own theological education, which took place just around the corner from Newman, at what was then called the United Faculty of Theology.

'I was fortunate to have studied in the heyday of ecumenism,' Frank said. 'In any class I was in, a third of the students might have been Jesuits, a third Anglican, a third Uniting Church – and there were quite a few lay people as well. And a lot of women. I was there with the first cohort of women who came through for ordination in the Anglican Church, some of whom are now bishops, like Kay Goldsworthy (current Archbishop of Perth). So it was a very rich, ecumenical and lively intellectual environment.'

By the time Frank began his theological education, he was already a Jesuit and a lawyer. To understand how this came about we need to jump back to 1971, when he started university in Queensland. It was, as he now puts it, a 'privileged time' to begin studying law and politics. That year, the Premier of Queensland, Sir Joh Bjelke-Petersen, had declared a State of Emergency so that the all-white Springbok rugby tour could proceed without protests. This raised big questions for a first-year law student: What is the role of law in society? Can a popularly elected government simply apply brute force or are there more fundamental questions at play? 'It was very fertile ground on which to be engaged,' says Frank, and he lost no time in getting involved. 'I was a very precocious undergraduate. Sir Zelman Cowen – a very distinguished jurist later to become Governor-General – was Vice-Chancellor of the university, and he always said that if anyone wanted to come and see him, they should, so I did. I read the riot act to him! I said given he was such a great constitutional lawyer, why wasn't more being said or done about the abuses going on in Queensland? Then, halfway through my first year at law school, Justice Richard Blackburn handed down a judgment in the Supreme Court of the Northern Territory that said Aboriginal people had no right to land.'

This legal statement had, and has, deep theological resonances. Frank once wrote an article with Dr Miriam-Rose Ungunmerr Baumann, an Aboriginal elder from Nauiyu who in 2021 was Senior Australian of the Year. In their article, they note that 'the Aboriginal reverence for the earth is born of 40,000 years' existence on the land, and more recently 200 years of dispossession and dispersal from the land'. For Aboriginal people, the land is a 'touchstone of the dreaming', and Aboriginal law 'is reverently recalled as belonging to the land'. The land remains – to use more European theological language – 'the sacramental expression of creation's life-giving power' for Aboriginal people. 'Living in ennobled equilibrium with the land,' Frank and Miriam write, 'Aborigines have continued to reverence their spirit place, abiding in its constancy, despite the whirlwind of change in which the West and the future immerse them.' For such a people to be denied rights to their own land, therefore, is traumatic in a way many Australians are yet to fully understand. It's a trauma Frank has tried hard to understand and, through the practice of law, to address.

The Justice Blackburn decision galvanised the young law student. The first Aboriginal legal service was soon set up in Brisbane and Frank started volunteering once a week. 'I helped out where I could and went along with people to court. I was being opened up to the lives of people suffering the effects of dispossession. Then in my final year at Queensland University in 1974, my father, who was a very senior barrister at the time, was appointed to represent Aboriginal people at the Woodward Royal Commission on land rights. When he came home from the hearings, our discussions helped me to reflect on the realities of what was going on.'

At this time, two themes of Frank Brennan's career were coming into focus: solidarity with the victims of injustice, and a belief in the power of the law to change things. Another theme emerged when Frank became a Jesuit. 'At the same time as I was studying law, I was also thinking of becoming a priest. I thought about being a diocesan priest and visited the seminary, but it wasn't for me. It was the kind of place where they played touch football five times a week on the lawn. I thought, I don't think I can do this! I'd been taught by the Missionaries of the Sacred Heart in Toowoomba and they had Aboriginal missions, so in 1974 I came down and visited the missionaries in Melbourne.' One of the future priests in training there was Pat Dodson, who later became a Labor Senator for Western Australia and a prominent Aboriginal activist. Pat told Frank he should check out the Jesuits. 'And I did. What impressed me was they said "you've been studying politics and law and you're good at those things. We don't quite know what we would do with you, but it would be good to have you aboard." If I'd become a diocesan priest or joined the Missionaries of the Sacred Heart, the attitude to my legal studies would have been, "that's all very well, but it's time to put all that behind you now and come and do the priestly thing." The Jesuits were open to my gifts being nurtured.'

It's a view of the priesthood that can be traced back to the founder of the Jesuits in 1534, Ignatius of Loyola. Ignatius was a former soldier who urged his followers to 'find God in all things'. Around the time Frank joined the order, Jesuits around the world were reflecting on what it meant to live out their calling in an unjust world. 'I had the good fortune to join around the time of the 32nd General Congregation of the Jesuits in Rome,' says Frank, 'which spelled out that the mission of the order was that critical relationship between faith and justice. The idea that you cannot profess the Christian faith unless you are also committed to justice – particularly for the poorest – and to reconciliation. All of that resonated strongly with me and spoke of the action of the Spirit in my life.'

Which brings us back to the question he posed to the students at Xavier: Which side of the river are we on? It's a question at the centre of Frank Brennan's theological vision. 'Part of our mission as Christians, I think,' says Frank, 'is to build a bridge across the river which allows people to move to either side, to have the capacity to stand on the side that is not familiar to us. I think that's the task that confronts us if we're to have a fuller theological sense of God's action in the world.' Crossing the river in this way led to Frank standing with Aboriginal people in some of their biggest legal battles, including *Mabo* – which resulted in the High Court saying that Aboriginal people do in fact have rights to land – and *Wik* – which said that native title rights could co-exist with pastoral leases. And alongside his work with Australia's oldest inhabitants came involvement with some of the newest: refugees and asylum seekers.

'I was directing the Jesuit Refugee Service in Dili in East Timor when *Tampa* happened,' he says. The *Tampa* was a Norwegian freighter ship carrying 433 asylum seekers who it had rescued at sea in Australian waters in 2001. Australia refused to offer asylum to those on board, and from Dili Frank heard that the Australian Government was in fact asking East Timor to take some of the refugees. 'This made me almost physically sick,' Frank says. 'I knew, and my government knew, that half the population of East Timor at that stage was either internally displaced or were refugees across the border in West Timor. The place had been destroyed. And here was Australia saying will you help us out? Sergio Vieira de Mello, who was head of the United Nations Transitional Administration in East Timor at the time, said this is just not on. The vehemency and simplicity of his response helped me realise just how morally bankrupt we had become as a nation. When I came back to Australia, I started visiting the asylum seeker detention centres at Woomera and at Baxter.'

This is another example of crossing the river to stand with people whose experiences were very different from Frank's own. But in doing so, he found he also needed to understand what it was like to be one of the people charged with making decisions about refugees in Australia. Frank remembers meeting a very senior public servant in the Department of Immigration. The public servant pointed out that, despite what the media was saying, Australia was and always had been a 'moderately generous country' in providing humanitarian places for people fleeing persecution. But he went on: 'There will always be *millions* of people fleeing persecution in the world. For us to be generous probably means a question of whether it's 20,000 or 30,000 or 40,000 a year. The question is, who's going to run the franchise? Us, or the people smugglers?'

Frank had similar challenging conversations with the Minister himself. 'Philip Ruddock would say to me, "It's all very well for you to say that this group of Afghans who have just turned up on a boat, all of whom are physically able young men who have been able to pay the money to get here, should take the place of the abused woman in the camp in Kenya".' Many activists would roll their eyes at this, but Frank takes the point seriously. 'There's never been a good answer to that concern. This has put me in a difficult space with some Church refugee groups and other advocates because I think their arguments are far too simplistic.'

But how do we know when to compromise and when not to? 'I think it's very important to be eyeballing both the decision-maker and the person adversely affected by the decision, because it stops you from becoming sanctimonious. The thing I can stand least in church social advocacy is people who have never in their lives spoken with a decision-maker, and who can't give the decision-maker the benefit of conscience. I think that is absolutely essential if you are to contribute to realistic political outcomes that are different to what they otherwise would have been.'

Frank is clear that Australia should be doing more for refugees. When we spoke, the US and its allies had recently abandoned Afghanistan to the Taliban. Scenes of suffering and fear were playing out every day in the news. Frank told us that in his view, 20,000 Afghan people should be settled in Australia. Why that number? 'One thousand for every year our soldiers were in Afghanistan.' Australia had recently announced we would take just 3000 Afghan refugees. 'That's an obscenity,' says Frank, 'particularly when you consider that we've dropped our total annual humanitarian intake to 11,750. The last time a competent report was done on these matters was the Houston report in 2012, which said our intake should immediately rise to 20,000, and that by now it should be 27,000.'

If his pragmatism on asylum seekers has sometimes caused tensions between Frank and some Christian social justice advocates, this is nothing compared to the reaction when he defended the right to a fair trial for the now late Cardinal George Pell, who in 2018 was charged with a number of historic child sex offences, found guilty, imprisoned, and finally exonerated and freed when the High Court quashed his convictions. This was, at first glance, an odd pairing. Cardinal Pell was seen as an arch-conservative in Church circles: a hardline defender of a particular vision of Catholic Christianity and an opponent of the kind of change that many in the Catholic Church, including Frank, are calling for. Frank Brennan and George Pell have often been at loggerheads; it would be hard to find two clergy in the Australian Catholic Church who were further apart on some theological issues. In fact, Cardinal Pell once commented publicly that 'part of the key to understanding Brennan is that he's not really educated in the Catholic tradition.'

Despite this slur and some serious ongoing theological differences, Frank became convinced that a serious injustice was being done to George Pell. He approached the issue as a lawyer. 'I attended the proceedings,' he says. 'I was one of the few people in the courtroom not only familiar with the way the law works, but also familiar with the way a Solemn High Mass works.' Pell was alleged to have abused two boys in a very short window of time after High Mass in his cathedral – something Frank believed was impossible as there would normally be dozens of people milling about. He is convinced the prosecution was motivated at least in part by a general disgust at the behaviour of the institutional church when it came to historic child sex abuse. 'The desire for a scapegoat, for a sacrificial lamb, existed not only in the wider community but also in the life of the church itself,' he says. 'Lots of people in the church would have been more than happy to see George Pell hung, drawn and quartered.'

But Frank's support of Pell came at a cost. 'One of the most hurtful things was that many of my fellow church people just said, "Oh, Frank's lost the plot. He's joined Team Pell". The theological differences between myself and George Pell are the same as they have ever been. But there's no doubt in my mind that George Pell was completely and utterly innocent of these charges.' As so often in his long career, Frank carved out an independent path. 'You have to remain true to yourself, try to find where the truth is, and put it out.'

On one feast day of St Ignatius of Loyola, founder of the Jesuits, Frank preached that we should 'commit ourselves afresh to choosing life, to acting for the glory of God, and to discerning the greater good in the midst of the minutiae of our lives, the failings of our church hierarchy, and the vapidity of our national politics

– all set against the vast horizon of the Kingdom to come and of the planet crying out for healing' (Brennan, *People's Quest*, 16). In the light of this vision, why should anyone consider studying theology today? 'For two reasons,' says Frank. 'Rowan Williams once said that theologians are those with trained minds who attest that nothing is off the table, that everything is to be subjected to absolute scrutiny, including whatever might be the underpinnings of the discipline. It's only theology that opens one to the fullness of that. The second is that I think it's only by studying theology, particularly going back to the Scriptures and the early church fathers, the tradition, that one has the opportunity – the privilege – of being able to get inside the minds of those who wrestled with the most fundamental of questions in their own social context, and that this can be studied in a way that transcends the prejudices of the moment in which we find ourselves now. So for me, I can't pretend to be a theologian, but an ongoing attention to the Scriptures and to the tradition helps to sustain me in maintaining what I think is a coherent plan of life.'

FURTHER READING

Frank Brennan, *Amplifying that Still, Small Voice*, ATF Press, 2015.

Frank Brennan, *Maintaining a Convinced and Pondered Trust: The 2015 Gasson Lectures*, ATF Press, 2015.

Frank Brennan, *Observations on the Pell Proceedings*, Connor Court Publishing, 2021.

Frank Brennan, *The People's Quest for Leadership in Church and State*, ATF Press, 2015.

Miriam Rose Ungunmerr-Baumann and Frank Brennan, 'Reverencing the earth in the Australian dreaming', *The Way* 32 (1989), 38-45.

Libby Byrne

Libby Byrne is an artist whose studio practice supports her capacity for creative engagement with people in a diverse range of therapeutic and pastoral care roles. She exhibits regularly in art galleries, healthcare and theological settings. For more than a decade, she has held an ongoing Academic Teaching and Research position with the Master of Art Therapy Program at La Trobe University. Prior to this, she worked as an art therapist with the Northern Centre Against Sexual Assault and in the Pastoral Care team at St Vincent's Public Hospital, with a focus on Palliative Care. Libby's PhD study was a Practice-led Theological inquiry into 'Healing Art and the Art of Healing' with a focus on her own experience of living with Multiple Sclerosis (MS).

SANCTUARY III, a painting by Libby Byrne, shows a human figure, female, curled almost in somersault, tumbling against a white background, cocooned in the light (a section of this work is reproduced on the cover of this book). There is a sense of shelter in the painting, like a womb, but also a sense of movement and growth. The figure moves in a place of creation and new creation. A place of healing. In the centre of the painting there is a crackling like electricity. Here the artist threw mustard seeds at the canvas – 'sort of as an infusion of faith,' she says.

When Libby Byrne was a teenager, the church she attended commissioned an artist to create a wall of stained glass; a large, abstracted image derived from a microscopic cross section of a blade of grass, to replace a series of nondescript opaque glass windows at the front of the church, behind the altar. After it was installed, the priest asked the congregation, who were worshipping in the light of this new image, what they saw. Libby says today that she 'was looking for something I was supposed to see. I felt like there must be a right answer.' She wrote down her answer and it was published in the church newsletter. 'It's embarrassing when I read it now,' she admits. 'It was what I thought was expected of me – such a small way of imagining the world.'

For Libby, art is now a much bigger way of imagining the world. For the past 25 years, she has been a working artist exhibiting regularly in and around Melbourne. She teaches and researches in the art therapy program at La Trobe University, and has worked with the Northern Centre Against Sexual Assault and in the Pastoral Care team at St Vincent's Public Hospital, with a focus on Palliative Care. When we spoke, she was preparing a new exhibition to be shown at the Queen Victoria Women's Centre in Melbourne, entitled *Being Among Trees*. In her notes to this show she says: 'as I make this work, I am becoming more deeply aware of the interdependence that shapes our life with trees ... As I learn to see the way trees live interdependently with one another, I see a healthy exchange between risk and power, shaping the way I can choose to live with other people.'

Several decades after she wrote her teenage reflections on the painting in her church, Libby Byrne returned to her home town to see the window again. It was a very different experience this time. She now had many years of practising art behind her, as well as many years working with others, through art, to find healing and wholeness. This time, as she observed the window behind the altar, 'I realised that I couldn't see it in one movement. My body kept moving in order to take it all in.' Then she realised something else: 'It resonated with what I had been painting for years when exploring images of God.' The image had stayed with her across the years and emerged in her own work. Several weeks later, Libby spoke to the priest who commissioned the window. Now retired, he told her that the church had wanted 'an image that you wouldn't be finished looking at in five minutes. People wouldn't quite understand it. They would keep being drawn back to look at it again, and not be finished with it.' The theological significance of this way of making and experiencing art is not lost on Libby: 'That's what art can help us do in a church,' she says. 'It can help draw us back to something we don't quite understand, but which we're compelled to return to – to see who God is in our lives, and not be finished with that in five minutes.'

'Something we don't understand but are compelled to return to' is a pretty good description of many people's experience of God – however they understand the term 'God'. Art, like theology, deals with mystery: things you can't say in a sentence or an article or a book. A mystery is something that must be encountered, not described or analysed. Theology, of course, does try to say things about the mystery of God – but language always strains at its limits, and when theology becomes a quest for certainty it has already lost its way.

Libby explains how she, as an artist, came to study theology. Working at the Centre Against Sexual Assault (CASA), she helped people who had experienced sexual assault to seek healing through art, listening to and speaking with these clients while they worked. 'I noticed,' she says, 'that if I worked long enough with people, they would often ask existential questions, questions about God, questions about how God could allow the assault to happen to them. Some people had even been abused in the church. I wasn't afraid to help people work through these questions, but I felt ill-equipped to do it. I needed some more theological training to help me understand how to help people with the deeper questions.' Following a calling to explore new ways of being with art and people in transformative places, she embarked on a course of studies that would eventually lead to a PhD.

Art deals with images; theology deals with images too. 'One thing I noticed when I started studying theology,' Libby says, 'was that the image we have of God permeates everything we believe about our faith. Is God a male figure overseeing everything, giving permission for this to happen, stopping that from happening? Is God a puppeteer? I realised that my role as an artist is to offer new and fresh images of God.'

Images might be said to lack the precision of words, and there is nervousness among some people of faith about the ambiguity, the shifting meanings, the interpretability of art. 'When I was studying art,' says Libby, 'I did a series of paintings called a life map exploring the shape of my inner and outer world over time and my experience of the presence of God in these places. I showed the minister of my church at the time and the series ended up hanging in the church.' The minister asked Libby for a quote from scripture to sit below the paintings. When she said she didn't have one, he asked if she could come up with one anyway. Why? 'People will want to know the authorial intent,' he said, which in this case did not actually involve a scripture reference. This was not the last time Libby experienced the pressure for an acceptable biblical 'explanation' of a work of art in church. But it is not always possible to retrofit scripture to a work of art; furthermore, it's not necessary. Art speaks for itself.

Theology can learn from art in this respect. There is room, in our engagement with God, for movement, for cautious approaches, sudden retreats, doubt, risk, trust, hope – the kind of experimentation and surprise that can be found in the practice of art. Theology is not a set of statements to be learned. It is an engagement with mystery; a straining towards what cannot be said.

Libby sometimes hears stories about how viewers respond to her work. A church invited Libby to paint the four women who are mentioned in the genealogy of Jesus in the Gospel of Matthew. 'When the priest in charge asked me to paint these women,' says Libby, 'I cried. I felt like I'd been preparing all my life to do something like this.' One of the women mentioned in the genealogy is Ruth, a non-Jew, who in the Bible story marries an Israelite and insists on remaining with her new people when he dies. She becomes the great-grandmother of King David who is – according to the early Christians – an ancestor of Jesus. Libby asked her then 18-year-old daughter to model for Ruth. She later overheard her daughter telling a friend that she had been in the studio, 'embodying' Ruth. 'I thought that was extraordinary,' says Libby. Her daughter had put her finger on the way that art can somehow make present that which it depicts. 'She knew that we had been together with Ruth in the studio.' To this day, people from the church where the paintings of the women hang contact Libby to tell her how important it is for them to sit near those women. 'These are abstracted figures, but they call people back. People are not finished with them.' This is art behaving more like theology than it ever could if it reached for a crudely propositional meaning.

After studying theology and continuing to work as an artist and art therapist, Libby felt she wanted to go deeper, and explore how her own artmaking practice and the material way in which she understood theology equipped her to work with people in the world. She was exploring ideas for a PhD when something unexpected happened. 'I had a few weeks off towards the end of the year in 2009 and was feeling tired and dizzy. By February, I had developed Optic Neuritis, and I was diagnosed with Multiple Sclerosis (MS).' MS is a chronic neurological disease which has no cure. The diagnosis was a deep shock, and the PhD was put on hold. 'I took a couple of years to recover from that first experience of illness. When I was ready to do the PhD, I realised that the best thing to do was to think about healing, and the experience I was now going through with MS.'

What is healing? We might conjure up visions of miracles, of people jumping out of wheelchairs, of crutches thrown away. Certainly the New Testament offers stories of Jesus healing people physically, even bringing the dead back to life. What are we to make of this today? It's a difficult question for any person of faith, but it becomes particularly acute when we or a loved one suffers a serious illness, particularly one with no cure. Libby points out that healing and cure are two different things. But this is a lesson often learned at great cost – unfortunately, sometimes it is not learned at all.

'Some faith traditions,' says Libby, 'say to people who are chronically ill, or who are dying, that if we pray hard enough, if we have enough faith, this will go away. This can be really devastating – I know people who have lived and died through that.' Libby worked in palliative care for three years. 'It makes their death so much more complicated because they aren't able to approach it knowing that it's going to happen. I've seen families left afterwards who just walk away from faith altogether. For me, the gift of working in palliative care was to realise just how real and normal it is for people to die.'

How can theology help people experience illness and mortality, without holding out empty hope for cures that may never come? 'We get very confused,' Libby says, 'about the difference between healing and cure. We think healing is about curing our medical ailments and illnesses. But to imagine that a cure is always possible is a form of denial, because essentially, we're all human and if we are living then we are also going to die. If we are cured of this particular illness, we will likely become ill with something else further down the track. If we're always looking for healing to rescue us from pain and cure our experience of illness, we risk rejecting the essential experience of being a human, who is both living and dying, with layers of pain and longing, resisting and accepting the other, simply living into the creative potential we all have for becoming whole and even healed.'

What then does it mean to be healed, if it is not to be cured? Libby would rather ask, what does it mean to be heal*ing*? 'Healed' has a full stop at the end,' she says. 'It's a state that is completed. But if I am heal*ing*, I am living into something that is still unfolding. Being healed is something I expect not to experience in this lifetime. But I hope to live in a way that is healing, to do things that are healing for me and others and move towards a state of being healed.'

Where does art fit in this process? Like theology at its best, art deals with uncertainty. In a recent paper, Libby discusses the phenomenon of 'therapeutic inertia', where clinicians treating long-term illnesses like MS become fixed in their methods and decisions, sometimes at the cost of their patients' health. Clinicians who don't like uncertainty are particularly susceptible to therapeutic inertia, says Libby, and art can help them move beyond this. 'Art is a way of developing our capacity to tolerate ambiguity,' she says. 'The clinician who can engage with art is more likely to avoid therapeutic inertia.' In this way, art contributes to the process of healing in the fullest sense.

The theologian Sarah Coakley developed a concept which she calls '*theologie totale*', which describes a theology that is fully engaged with science, philosophy, the social sciences and art. As an artist, how does Libby experience the relationship between theology and the arts today? 'I think artists are doing it,' says Libby, 'but the church is not necessarily seeing it. There are a lot of artists who are exploring the ideas and questions that systematic theologians explore, but because artists are not saying they're theologians, the church doesn't notice it going on. People have been siloed. You're an artist, or you're a theologian, or you're a therapist. I have even encountered silos existing between my work as an artist painting theology and what is described as religious art.'

'Often, for churches,' she goes on, 'art is just there to illustrate something the church wants people to understand. But for art to do what Sarah Coakley is wanting it to do, we have to allow the artist to say, look, there is no scripture attached to this – this is just my experience of being in the world.' And then to ask the question:

'Do you see Christ in this?' Not only does the church need to allow artists to ask this question, says Libby, 'but also scientists and others, as well as marginalised voices, people who have been abused or victimised by the church. We have to allow people to ask a question, rather than just make a statement. Theology often starts with a question.' We should allow more voices to be heard, she says, if we want the full picture: 'Every voice is unique. We can't expect one voice to tell a story that will fit with everyone's experience. Until we've heard everyone's voice, there are voices missing.'

Both theology and art open up questions rather than shutting them down; they increase our ability to sit with mystery and ambiguity as we approach God. Both disciplines should be more fully welcomed into the life of the church. Libby says: 'After studying theology, I am saddened by how few of the things I've learned and explored with art have been able to filter back into the church. I grieve that, to be honest, because I think there are many people who need to hear and know that there are different ways of thinking about the questions that call their attention and shape their experience of living faith in the world. We would all be enriched if new images of God, and new ways of seeing and being together in faith were welcome in church.'

FURTHER READING

Libby Byrne website: libbybyrne.com.au

Libby Byrne, 'Unless Something Goes Wrong: Making Art to Understand and Mitigate the Risk of Therapeutic Inertia in the Treatment of Multiple Sclerosis' in *Journal of Patient Experience*, (10) (2023)

Sarah Coakley, *God, Sexuality, and the Self: An Essay 'On the Trinity'*, Cambridge University Press, 2013

Dan Fleming

Dan Fleming is head of ethics for St Vincent's Health Australia, a role which sees him leading ethics education, advice, and strategy across the St Vincent's Health Australia network. Dan is also Adjunct Professor of Ethics for the School of Medicine at the University of Notre Dame, Australia. Dan holds a PhD in moral philosophy and theology and is the author of over 50 academic and media publications in the areas of moral philosophy, theological ethics, healthcare ethics, and moral education. In 2018-19, Dan led Catholic Health Australia's response to the Voluntary Assisted Dying Act in Victoria, a collaborative response among all Catholic Health and Aged Care services in Victoria to the new legislation.

'WHEN YOU DO A THEOLOGY DEGREE,' says Dan Fleming, 'you don't think you're going to end up in a tense interview on national TV because of it.'

Dan Fleming's theology is inseparable from his personal and professional life. As Group Manager of Ethics and Formation at St Vincent's Health Australia, he needs it every day. In 2017, Victoria introduced new Voluntary Assisted Dying (VAD) laws – which enabled eligible people with terminal illnesses to end their own lives at a time of their choosing. This was a difficult moment for the Catholic health care sector. Though deeply invested in end of life care, VAD was not something they could practise, as it conflicted with their beliefs in human dignity and the ethical practice of medicine. But the law was introduced, and Catholic health care services had to figure out how to uphold their commitments to dying patients on the one hand and their objection to VAD on the other. Dan was asked to lead the process of formulating a response, which made him grateful for his theological training. When he first embarked upon a PhD, he says, 'I had no idea of the significance of it. But I use it at work literally every single day.' And it's what landed him on ABC News Breakfast.

So how did it all begin?

Dan was raised in New South Wales by a loving father and mother who were both in the radio industry. He went to church with his mother most weeks, and to a Catholic school. 'The Church was around me but never really within me,' he says. 'I always found faith a safe, comfortable place to be, but more as a background than a foreground.' As many do, Dan started asking the big questions at high school: 'I went through a dark spot,' he says, 'which led to a bit of a hunt for meaning.'

Meaning was found, at first, not through books but through a person. 'There was a wonderful chaplain at the school,' Dan explains, 'a Polish priest from a religious order called the Salvatorians. He helped me see a different face of the church; to understand the Christian faith not as a background, but as a context in which one could meet God.'

At World Youth Day in 2002, Dan did meet God. For the uninitiated, World Youth Day is a massive global Catholic event held somewhere in the world every few years. Tens of thousands of young Catholics gather to worship and learn together. In Canada in 2002, the theme of World Youth Day came from the fifth chapter of Matthew: 'You are the salt of the earth. You are the light of the world.' Dan attended and was, in his words, 'profoundly transformed.'

Then came university. Theology did not really seem like an option; as the son of a radio engineer and a copywriter, he was drawn to something that had a more practical edge. Dan started a Bachelor of Education, focused on technology and computing. But there was a pull from elsewhere. 'I kept walking past the theology classes and thinking they sounded so much better than what I was doing! So I jumped ship into a Bachelor of Theology.'

It's commonplace today to describe theology as 'faith seeking understanding', an expression adapted from St Anselm's exhortation to all Christians to engage their senses and talents as fully as possible with their beliefs, including their use of reason. When Dan's experience of God at World Youth Day was brought into contact with formal theology, 'I really did fall in love with it,' he says. 'I was okay academically throughout school, but I really came alive in this space.' It wasn't just the content. Just as his chaplain's pastoral care had helped him in high school, so Dan's experience of studying theology was shaped by the people who taught it: 'My lecturers were eminently pastoral people,' he says. 'They witnessed to something beautiful and true in the way they taught and the way they lived.'

When it came time to do a PhD, Dan's practical bent came once again to the fore. 'I come from a practical family,' he says. 'When it comes to ideas, I'm mainly interested in what they mean for how we go about life. The work of theory is critical, and has its own integrity. But it's never just a thought exercise for me.' The obvious place to start a PhD thesis was with a practical ethical question. But Dan soon came to realise that the questions he was interested in required him to ask other questions: deeper, more fundamental questions about God, humanity and the world.

'A common understanding of Catholic ethics is one that starts with specific moral teachings, about specific actions,' Dan tells us. 'But those rest on much deeper considerations, which shed light on other salient elements of a question.' For example: 'The abuse crisis in the church raises questions about specific actions, especially how people entrusted with ministry could treat children so appallingly. But it also raises more fundamental questions about mutual responsibility, and why so many in the church didn't appreciate their responsibilities to one another, particularly to those whose dignity was most at risk.' Or, to return to VAD, 'On the one hand, this is about whether intentionally bringing about someone's death is the right thing when they are suffering at the end of life. But the practice also raises more fundamental questions about the purpose of medicine, and what society owes to those who are suffering.'

Thinking about mutual responsibility – what we owe one another – led Dan to investigate the work of a Jewish philosopher, Emmanuel Levinas, who wrote about the origins of our ethical responsibility to one another as human beings. Levinas is a phenomenologist – that is, a philosopher who pays careful attention to the ways in which we experience the world, the ways things present themselves to us, the ways phenomena are 'given' to our experience. In Levinas Dan found a new way of thinking about what lies behind ethics; how an appreciation of our radical responsibility for one another animates our conscience, even before we come to this or that ethical decision. 'Levinas gives a phenomenological account of conscience,' Dan explains, 'which is very much aligned with a Christian ethic of conscience as something that is given, something primordial.' Quoting from the Second Vatican Council's document *Gaudium et spes*, Dan notes that conscience understood in this way is 'the voice of God echoing in our hearts.' Our answer to this echo in the deepest part of who we are manifests in the way we live, and the way we respond to particular ethical questions. 'Ethics is not about this or that issue,' says Dan, 'but rather about the fundamental posture of the human person. It changes the way you see everything.' That's true of individuals, but Dan also adds: 'If you can bring this into an organisation it can produce a very significant shift of mindset.'

So Dan, who found himself meeting God experientially at World Youth Day in 2002, was now armed with a PhD in theological ethics, one which understood ethics as grounded in the voice of God in the human heart. Where to from here? Dan says an academic career was 'very much the trajectory and the dream' at this point. He had loved the idea of communicating theology to students ever since his first theology class. 'The lecturer in my first class read the first sentences of Genesis in the original Hebrew. Within 20 minutes he'd told us a whole lot of stuff I'd never heard before. I thought, gosh – that's what I want to do.'

That's what he did do for a while, teaching theology and ethics at the Broken Bay Institute (BBI) in Sydney. He liked the practical focus of the place: 'BBI was filled with practical and pastoral people who always wanted to know, how does this apply? The team there wanted to support their students in working through the practical application of theology. There I began working with people in healthcare. They were interested in what a theology offered when they had a dying patient in front of them. Or what difference a theological worldview makes for a health executive facing a major budget deficit?'

Then came a tap on the shoulder. Dan had been doing a lot of work with the Catholic health sector, helping staff gain a deeper understanding of the Catholic ethical tradition, and what it means to keep that tradition alive today. He found he was good at communicating theological ideas in ways that made sense in a contemporary context. 'I was speaking about old things in a new way.'

Eventually, he was approached by St Vincent's Health Australia, who invited him to keep doing what he was doing within their organisation. 'I didn't really have to think about it', he says. 'St Vincent's is known for keeping the Catholic ethical tradition alive and at its best.' This had been true for a long time: 'Their response to HIV-AIDS in the eighties and nineties, for example – that's where Catholic ethics was lived out in the most profound ways.' Dan seized the opportunity to bring his experience from the world of the academy and to start grappling with the live ethical questions faced by working hospitals around the country.

The organisation that is now St Vincent's Health Australia was started by a handful of vowed religious – the Sisters of Charity – in 1893. Its mission to this day is 'to express the love of God to those in need through the healing ministry of Jesus.' For Dan, this can't be allowed to become an empty slogan, or a bit of history. 'If we don't remain intentional about it,' he says, 'then we become like any other organisation. To be true to who we are, our mission has to live in a dynamic way: it's about more than the names of our hospitals, the values we've got on the wall, or the money we set aside for charitable work. It's about where we stand, why we stand there, who we're standing with, and how we respond to the suffering of those entrusted to our care. That's the healing ministry of Jesus – that's the treasured mission we're challenged to continue. We're asked to be more than our history or our words.'

What does it mean to be more? For Dan, during the VAD debate, it meant trying to communicate the fullness of the Catholic position to an often sceptical public. 'Euthanasia is something that's categorically ruled out in Catholic ethics,' he explains. 'Almost everything's on the table for us when it comes to end of life care – but directly and intentionally ending life isn't.' Before long, it was clear that mainstream public opinion was not with the Catholic Church on this issue. The law changed, but this was not the end of the matter. 'It was no longer about trying to convince policymakers about what we ought to do as a community,' says Dan. 'Now it was a question of – given this legislation – how do we respond with integrity? As a true reflection of who we are?'

This is where the importance of theology becomes clear: when a change in the world forces new thinking about how to apply old ideas – like the dignity of every human life – to new situations. Dan got to work leading his team through these questions. 'Our whole project,' says Dan, 'was led from a deep theological framework. We went back to Biblical texts, we went back through the history of the Sisters of Charity and the other Catholic orders who established similar ministries in Australia, asking: who are we called to be in the face of the dying patient?' Even more difficult: 'How should we respond to a patient at one of our facilities who is actively engaged in the pursuit of VAD?'

There was a lot of history to draw from. 'The Sisters of Charity set up the country's first dedicated end of life service in 1890,' Dan says. These particular Sisters have always been willing to get their hands dirty in the mess of a suffering world. In the 1990s, they put their hand up to run a safe injecting facility for drug users in Sydney, until they were stopped by the Vatican. Even earlier, in the nineteenth century, they shocked some of the local church hierarchy by providing *Protestant* prayer books for patients in their Catholic hospital. 'This hospital is for everyone,' they insisted. The Sisters went to rough Kings Cross bars with collecting tins raising money for health services. They were, and are, a fiercely practical order focused on the needs of the people in front of them, sometimes in conflict with church authorities.

Inspired by the Sisters of Charity and their history, Dan wondered how a Catholic hospital should respond when someone wanted to take their own life by means of VAD. He wrote an article raising the possibility that Catholic clinicians or pastoral workers or priests could be present when someone took this step; the Vatican's Congregation for the Doctrine of the Faith had suggested they couldn't. 'The question I asked is: if we really believe in our approach to end of life care, shouldn't we witness to that even in the most difficult circumstances, by being there? While someone is in our care, they might go about something we don't agree with, but it doesn't mean we change the care we offer them.' It's a compelling image, one that resonates with the complex actions of Jesus Christ recorded in the gospels.

The Catholic health sector continues to struggle with questions around VAD; and this will not be its last challenge in a changing world. Dan says Christian organisations need to approach these issues constructively. 'The risk is we get into a reactive posture: we say, well, we just don't do that here. Or we just kind of cower in the corner and shut the door and hope there are no conflicts.' Neither is good enough. Engagement is needed, and this can only be done with adequate theological preparation. 'We created an approach to VAD,' says Dan, 'that was deeply founded on our ethic of care, deeply embedded within a theological framework.' And, he laughs, 'it even stood up to some pretty aggressive questioning on national TV!'

Dan Fleming wrote another article at the height of the VAD debate asking, 'according to what narrative is VAD an expression of the virtue of compassion?' His answer: neoliberalism. This way of thinking about the world 'prioritises the construction of the individual self largely in entrepreneurial terms and set aside from connections to tradition, history and community' and 'casts suspicion on any form of dependency on others.'

This is one task of theology: to uncover and interrogate the assumptions that lie behind current debates. If our only way of thinking about questions of life and death comes from neoliberalism, says Dan, then we are likely to conclude that protecting human dignity can sometimes mean purposely ending someone's life. But if we reject the neoliberal frame, we can prioritise other commitments: 'to always comfort and accompany; to never abandon; to offer fully sufficient pain relief, even if that has the effect of hastening the end of a person's life; and to honour requests to withdraw or withhold treatments that a person wishes to withdraw or withhold, or which have become overly burdensome.'

Uncovering assumptions also includes examining the structures of society, and not just their consequences. The theological concept of 'structural sin' becomes helpful here. This refers to the ways in which the structures of organisations, or indeed of whole societies, can do harm to vulnerable people within them. But academic theology can only do so much when it comes to understanding structural sin. Much of what can be learnt can only be learnt through the experience of standing with those who suffer. 'One only begins to see the structure of sin,' says Dan, 'when one stands with the people who are actually impacted by it. There's a theological imperative in the Christian tradition to get out there and stand with those who suffer.'

Dan has been thinking, for example, about how the law responds to people who use illicit drugs. 'From one perspective, our current criminalisation of injecting drug users sounds perfectly reasonable,' he says. 'But standing with those people and seeing how that response compounds other injustices and makes life impossible, really starts to show up the reality that something that was perhaps well-intentioned is not serving the good and should be changed.' Based on this stance, Dan co-led a process of discernment on this issue at St Vincent's – drawing in the insights of experts in caring for those who take drugs, people with lived experience, and many others – which ultimately led to St Vincent's offering its voice in support of drug law reform.

What are the implications of all this for theological education?

'There's a huge need for theology,' says Dan. 'But my fear is that the need, the relevance, isn't seen.' Why? Dan points to a crisis of trust in religion and in the churches, especially following the sex abuse crisis. He thinks this can be addressed. 'Sometimes I find the church falls into a way of thinking which suggests that the "world" won't listen to us. Christians claim of society that everyone's bound up in their ideologies, and can't see the truths that we can see.' If that's the case, Dan asks, 'what place is there for theology?' But he also suggests that's too convenient an explanation, which doesn't account for the ways the problem might be 'in here' rather than 'out there': perhaps we're not communicating in a way that makes sense to those we want to listen to us. 'I'm yet to meet someone who hears the story of St Vincent's and doesn't what to know more. Why did these women set up this amazing organisation? Why does it keep doing this amazing work? There's a doorway into appreciating the place of theology, right there.' Dan credits his extensive theological education with helping him communicate theological ideas simply and to diverse audiences. 'The more you're in touch with the depth of the literature the more you are able to explain it clearly. The more you go deep with the material the more it can sort of spill out.'

What's Dan's top tip for communicating theology? 'The best thing I have at my fingertips,' he says, 'is a litany of parables. Not only the parables of Jesus, but the parables of the Sisters of Charity. Almost every day, I come across a story about the Sisters and think, I can't believe they did that!' He comes back to the early Sisters insisting that Protestant prayer books be available in the hospital. 'How does this help us think about different groups who might feel excluded from a Catholic hospital today? This is historical theology and theological ethics at once. Learning about how theology was lived out by these remarkable women.'

A theologian has to be an archaeologist, digging beneath current attitudes, exposing and questioning what is fundamental. 'There are some big faith systems at play today which really aren't good,' says Dan. 'Bringing a worldview credibly to the table is central for the common good. Otherwise we end up blind to the structures of sin which can radically undermine human dignity.'

He names some other issues in health care that theology will need to deal with in the not too distant future: artificial intelligence, biotechnology, addiction, public health crises. None of these will be easy to address. 'Courage is probably the virtue I struggle with most,' Dan admits. 'But what enables me to be courageous is remembering to whom I answer. It's not a board of trustees, it's not a government – it's our God.'

FURTHER READING

Daniel Fleming, *Attentiveness to Vulnerability: A Dialogue Between Emmanuel Levinas, Jean Porter, and the Virtue of Solidarity*, Wipf and Stock, 2019

Daniel Fleming, 'The compassionate state? Voluntary Assisted Dying, neoliberalism and the problem of virtue without an anchor', *ABC Religion and Ethics*, March 2019

Fleming, D. Keenan, J. and Zollner, H (editors) *Facing the Sexual Abuse Crisis in the Church: Perspectives from Theology and Theological Ethics* Pickwick, 2023. Full text available online at https://jmt.scholasticahq.com/issue/6906

Fleming, D. & Carter, D. (editors) *'Voluntary Assisted Dying': Law? Health? Justice?* ANU Press, 2022. Full text available online at https://press.anu.edu.au/publications/voluntary-assisted-dying

Fleming, D. 'Inequalities and bioethics in public health during Covid-19: An Australian perspective' in *Concilium* 2022 (2), 66-77 (2022)

Fleming, D. 'Is Presence Always Complicity? An Analysis of Presence, Its Moral Objects and Scandal in Proximity to Physician Assisted Suicide and Euthanasia' in *Theological Studies*, 82 (3), 487-508 (2021)

Fleming, D. 'Beyond the Abuse of Power and the Abuse of Conscience: Charting a Course for Theological Ethics in Response to the Sexual Abuse Crisis in the Australian Catholic Church' in *Asian Horizons*, 14 (2), 333-346 (2020)

Fleming, D. 'Appropriation, Australia's Drinking Problem, and the Cost of Resistance in Catholic Health Services' in *Journal of Moral Theology*, 9 (2), 15-38 (2020).

ANNE PATTEL-GRAY

Anne Pattel-Gray is a descendant of the Bidjara/Kari Kari people of Queensland and a celebrated Aboriginal leader. Throughout her career, she has exercised numerous leadership and consultancy roles in First Nations organisations and not-for-profit agencies. In 1995, Professor Pattel-Gray was the first Aboriginal person to be awarded a PhD at the University of Sydney, published as The Great White Flood: Racism in Australia. *She has held Visiting Professorships at Gurukul Theological Seminary, Harvard University and Otago University. From 2022 to 2024 she was Professor of Indigenous Studies and Head of the School of Indigenous Studies at the University of Divinity.*

ANNE PATTEL-GRAY'S theological education began, literally, at her mother's knee. As a young child in Sunday School one morning at her family's Methodist church in Townsville, she listened as the teacher told the children about the 'curse of Ham'. In the book of Genesis, one of Noah's sons, Ham, 'saw his father's nakedness' (we don't know exactly what this means but it is assumed to involve a shameful act of some kind), and is told by Noah that Ham's own son will be cursed and will be a 'servant of servants' forever. The story of Ham runs for just a few lines, without mention of either race or skin colour, but for centuries white Christians used this text to justify the oppression and enslavement of black people, who were said to be the descendants of Ham, the 'cursed race'.

It's hard to imagine how such an inept and incoherent interpretation of a scriptural passage was able to gain such traction, but it did, and caused untold damage over the centuries. Anne's

Sunday School teacher did not bring up the story in order to denounce this wrong interpretation, but to endorse it. As Anne sat among the other children that day, she felt every eye turning to look at her. 'We were the only black family in the church,' she says today. 'Honestly, if I could have prayed to God to open the earth and swallow me up, I would have. Tears formed in my eyes. I just wanted to be invisible.' And a question formed in her mind: 'How can people who call themselves Christians hate me so much, just because of the colour of my skin?'

As soon as church ended, Anne got into the family car and wept. Her mother asked what was wrong. 'Mum, why do white people hate us so much?' she said. 'I'm created by God the same as they are. Why am I less than them? Why did God make me black?' This must have been a painful question for a mother to hear, but her response was powerful. 'You are created by the Creator,' she said. 'And you are created in the image of God which makes you magnificent. Your being Aboriginal doesn't make you less than any white person on this planet.' Anne remembers her mother's words clearly. 'You are equal. Always remember that, child. You are equal to anyone who walks on this planet because you are a child of God, created by the same Creator.'

Still the ten-year-old Anne was not satisfied. 'But why do they hate us?' Her mother told her that as she got older, she would understand. 'They have every reason to justify their hatred of us because they stole our land,' her mother went on. 'They massacred our people. They took our children. They denied us our language, our culture. They hate themselves so they've got to hate someone else more than themselves. We become the point of their hatred because we remind them of what they've done.'

'It took me many years to understand that,' Anne says today. 'But that was where my theological journey began. That was when I started to question the Bible, or at least the interpretation that

Westerners had of the Bible. I began to read it through First Nations eyes, through Aboriginal eyes, to see what the Bible had to say that was affirming to me.'

Anne Pattel-Gray is a descendant of the Bidjara/Kari Kari people in Queensland, and a renowned scholar, theologian and activist. The theological journey she describes led to her becoming the first Aboriginal woman to complete a PhD at Sydney University (in 1995), to the writing of several books and many articles, to guest lectures at prestigious theological institutions in places like Harvard and Oxford, and to job offers from around the world. She was Professor and Chair of Department at United Theological College in Bangalore, India, from 1998 to 2001. She could in fact have spent her entire career overseas. 'I was offered a position at Harvard,' Anne says, 'but I knocked it back. I said, I didn't get a PhD to come over here. I got it to make a difference in Australia. That's where the fight is for me.'

But it hasn't been easy. 'I've been pretty marginalised in this country at times and pretty lonely.' Anne was the founding executive secretary of the Aboriginal and Islander Commission of the National Council of Churches. She was also, in the words of her former PhD supervisor, Professor Gary Trompf, 'the first to bring the details of the Stolen Generations to a large international forum, at the meeting of the World Council of Churches in Canberra in 1991.' From 2022 to 2024 Anne was Professor of Indigenous Studies at the University of Divinity. She is currently completing a book on her 'Red Ochre Theology'.

Anne Pattel-Gray has a message other Australians need to hear, particularly those of us involved in theological education. The uncomfortable reality is that Christians have been complicit in a gross betrayal of the gospel truth that Anne learned from her mother, which is that every single person is made in the image of the Creator and every person is sacred on that basis and worthy of respect. That insight is the mirror image of the prevailing colonial assumption that all people are not equal. The British invasion of Australia could not have happened in the way that it did if it were not for what Anne calls 'the biggest legal lie ever constructed' – *terra nullius* – the claim that the land mass discovered by Captain Cook was 'nobody's land' and therefore up for grabs.

If the land was 'nobody's', then the people living on the land were 'nobodies' and were treated as such. 'Colonial society is founded on racist ideology,' Anne says, 'and it permeates all aspects of that society: government, media, education, health, courts, prisons, you name it.' Anne's message would be easier to hear if the effects of the racism she describes were confined to the past. But as she reminds us, 'we still see the benefits of colonialism for white people, and the costs to Aboriginal people who are disenfranchised as a result.'

Not only has theology been complicit in colonialism, it has been used to inspire and support it. In her book *The Great White Flood*, Anne writes that 'the Australian Church believed, propagated and implemented a theology that was heretical, as it did not search for the ultimate truth but rather stopped short in the netherworld of racism, genocide and oppression against Australian Aboriginal People.' She adds, 'theological heresy became theological imperialism, which in turn became heretical practice and blasphemy.'

'I quite often struggle with the Old Testament,' Anne admits, 'because of the colonial interpretation that has been placed on it. To justify genocide, theft of land, oppression, the denial of the humanity of First Nations people, and so on.' She questioned this early on. 'I began to say, this can't be right. Surely this Bible that I'm reading, like most history, is written by the victors, and the stories of those who are oppressed or marginalised or victimised are silenced?'

Anne looked around for voices saying similar things. Aboriginal leaders from the 1960s had 'made clear for the Aboriginal Christian ... that they themselves, through their lived experience with God from time immemorial, had direct access to God, and that their relationship to Jesus Christ was established a long time before the white invasion of their land' (Pattel-Gray, 'Methodology'). She also looked beyond Australia's shores. 'The more I got involved with First Nations people around the globe,' Anne says, 'the more I realised that we had been hoodwinked in Australia. Our people had been lied to by the church. They delivered biblical interpretations to justify their colonial oppression and their theft and lies. That just got me really angry. Not to the point of explosion; not wanting to attack; but wanting to expose the hypocrisy. That began my journey and I've been on it ever since.'

It hasn't been an easy journey, because it is not an easy message. Anne encountered resistance from the start. 'For my PhD,' she says, 'I wanted to look at racism from a theological perspective. I wanted to look at the impact of biblical interpretations on the missions that were done to Aboriginal people.' She examined the work of missionaries in the Victorian period. 'In society, particularly in the church, we glorify these people. We hold them up as pillars of our society. But when I looked into them, what I found was shocking.'

She gives the example of a Catholic priest in the Tiwi Islands north of Darwin, who became determined to stop promised marriages. Promised marriages involve complex relationships between various kinship groups and are an important part of many traditional Aboriginal societies; but for the Church, or at least for this priest, they were associated with the kind of 'paganism' that Christianity had come to stamp out. But the Tiwi Island people, Anne says, 'were clever because they ended up pulling the wool over his eyes.' How? 'They took the marriage lines underground. When two people had been promised to one another in the traditional way and came to marrying age, they'd say to the priest, oh Father,

I think such and such is sweet on such and such – don't you think they would make a good match? And they held together all their marriage lines, all their clan groups, all their protocols without this man even having a clue what they were doing.' The end of the story reveals a typical pattern of the time: 'The Catholic Church thought he had destroyed the Aboriginal culture,' says Anne, 'and made him Bishop of Darwin as a reward.'

She tells the story of another Christian minister, this time in Yarrabah, Queensland. This was a man held up as a role model for Christians, a great missionary. But he was a married man with children who also fathered several other children to an Aboriginal woman. 'These children were never claimed by him,' says Anne, 'but they wear his name to this day. And this is someone we want to hold up as a great man! These were the kinds of things I was exposing to the church.'

It did not go down well. 'Lo and behold,' says Anne, 'the old patriarchy within the religious studies department suddenly wanted me to show cause as to why I should be allowed to continue with my PhD.' There could be no question about the academic quality of her work. 'My book *The Great White Flood*, which came from my PhD, has over 300 original footnotes, not secondary sources. It was well sourced, well researched, well argued.' It's not hard to figure out precisely what about the work made people upset. It was shattering some long-held, and comfortable, assumptions about our Christian history in Australia. As Anne said to the academic panel at Sydney University: 'It's only the truth. How can I be criticised for the truth?' In the end, her supervisor, Garry Trompf, defended Anne. 'He even got the Vice-Chancellor to defend me. I wouldn't have been awarded my PhD if it wasn't for him.'

Anne's life and career offer both negative and positive lessons for theology. Those of us who think theology can be a force for good must also acknowledge its potential for evil. Many of the assumptions that underlay the oppression of First Nations people in Australia were, at base, theological. Theological ideas are powerful even when they are wrong. Adding 'thus saith the Lord' to a claim makes it hard to argue with. Theologians (and for that matter anyone who preaches) need to remember they are playing with fire. But as Anne Pattel-Gray also reminds us, the answer to bad theology is not no theology at all, but a better one – and a better theology is possible. Anne's own work is an example of this. 'As I grew up,' says Anne, 'my culture affirmed my relationship with the Creator.' And today? 'My theology is what sustains me. Without it, I wouldn't have been able to survive. I wouldn't be here today if it wasn't for my theology and my relationship with the Creator.'

Aboriginal theology is about relationship and interconnection between people, and between people and land. 'The Creator bestowed land to us,' says Anne, 'to each language group, to care for, to watch over, to live with, to protect. Everything we wanted was given to us. We didn't need capitalism. We didn't need industrialisation. We had the Creator living with us. We had to work hard to find a feed. But a lot of our time was taken up in religious activities. Making sure the laws the Creator gave us were lived every day. They weren't something we put on and then took off. Aboriginal people see ourselves as a vessel to honour the Creator. Everything we do in creation, with each other, in economics – it informs every aspect of our life.'

How can we get more Aboriginal theology into the mainstream discourse? 'My vision is to impact every seminary in this country, no matter what denomination, to make Aboriginal theology, missiology, spirituality a component of every degree for every student.' Anne wants our future ministers, theologians and biblical scholars to be instruments of change. In the past, Aboriginal studies at Australian universities left a lot to be desired. 'Universities always had their so-called Aboriginal experts,' says Anne. These experts often didn't even understand Aboriginal languages, but it didn't seem to matter. Even today, 'Aboriginal people aren't seen as the experts in academia: white people are the experts. We need to elevate more Aboriginal people in the academic world and recognise their authority.'

But can theology really make a difference today? Anne insists that it can. 'Don't be doubting,' she says. 'Believe in a powerful God. People are searching for something and someone to believe in. Theology provides hope. It not only provides justice, it not only holds people accountable, it not only calls us to have obligations to each other, to the earth, to everything. It also calls us to be innovative and to inspire. To start lifting each other up and seeing what's good in each other. Affirming each other's humanity. There's no other methodology, other than theology, that can bring about transformation. We've got to get back to basics. We've forgotten who the Creator is, we've forgotten to honour the Creator.'

Transforming theology can also help transform the country. Anne is a strong supporter of the Uluru Statement from the Heart – a profoundly theological statement – which not only calls for 'the establishment of a First Nations Voice enshrined in the Constitution', but also a 'Makarrata Commission to supervise a process of agreement-making between governments and First Nations and truth-telling about our history.' Anne encourages people of faith to welcome the statement in full. 'The recognition in a treaty,' she says, 'does not take from you what you own. It deconstructs the colonial system that has disenfranchised black people in this country and benefited and given privilege to white people. Everybody can gain. Everybody can have wealth. Everybody can have privilege and education. There shouldn't be a child dying in this country because they can't get medical care. There shouldn't be child that's illiterate because they can't get a great education. The statistics of First Nations are damning, absolutely damning.'

But Anne Pattel-Gray has hope. Without it, she could not have continued her work for so many years in what has often been a hostile environment. Her hope is grounded in theology – and hope is what theology is for. One thing we can hope for is that future Aboriginal children will never have to feel what Anne felt sitting in that Sunday School classroom all those years ago. If this comes true, it will be partly due to the work of people like Anne. Her work will not always win her friends. 'You either love me or you hate me,' she says, 'but you can't be indifferent, because I provoke emotion. I want emotion, because it means we're having the conversation, whatever that conversation might be.'

There is grace in Anne Pattel-Gray's words, even if it is a confronting grace, a demanding grace, a grace that asks us to listen to uncomfortable truths and perhaps respond in unfamiliar ways. But it is grace nonetheless because underlying her entire worldview is love. 'It all comes back to love,' says Anne. 'Love is what transforms. The basic principles of theology are about love. We are all created in the image of the Creator. The Creator doesn't make mistakes. How do we find that gift that each of us brings to the table of humanity?'

FURTHER READING

Anne Pattel-Gray, *Through Aboriginal Eyes: The Cry from the Wilderness*, WCC Publications, 1991

Anne Pattel-Gray, *The Great White Flood: Racism in Australia*, Scholars Press, 1998

Anne Pattel-Gray, 'Methodology in an Aboriginal Theology' in *The Cambridge Companion to Black Theology*, Cambridge University Press, 2012, 278-297.

Tony Rinaudo

Tony Rinaudo is a Natural Resources Management Specialist and agronomist working for World Vision Australia. Over 25 years ago, working with local farmers in Niger, he began implementing a conservation farming system now known as Farmer Managed Natural Regeneration (FMNR). This approach has been applied in 29 countries globally and has empowered and inspired a farmer-led movement across continents, regreening the lands, improving the livelihoods of millions and helping to combat climate change.

As a child, Tony Rinaudo remembers staring at hills stripped bare of trees near his parent's home in Myrtleford, in north-eastern Victoria. It was timber country and there was also farming of tobacco and other crops. Tony felt strange playing with his friends in imported pine forests, planted on cleared bushland, with their eerie silence and scant animal life. 'It was green, but a green desert,' he says. The hills left bare also seemed wrong in a way he could not yet articulate. 'I felt angry. I felt frustrated. I was never good with words. And I didn't know what positive steps I could take. I didn't know how I could make a difference.'

He found a way to make a difference, but it took a lifetime of hard work, and much struggling in prayer. In 2018, Tony Rinaudo won a Right Livelihood Award – sometimes called the 'alternative Nobel Prize' – an award set up to 'honour and support courageous people solving global problems'. Tony was honoured for 'demonstrating on a large scale how drylands can be greened at minimal cost, improving the livelihoods of millions of people.'

Today, Tony is known worldwide as the 'Forest Maker'. His re-greening method is called Farmer Managed Natural Regeneration, or FMNR. It is a way of regrowing trees and shrubs from their stumps or root systems and from self-sown native seeds – which sounds simple, but is having a profound effect on swathes of degraded land across Africa and beyond, while at the same time transforming the lives of the people who live there. When trees are restored, they improve the soil, reduce erosion, help to purify and often increase local water supplies and bring animals back to the area. Crop yields increase, and more timber becomes available for local people to use.

With FMNR, livestock have more fodder and can be tended under the newly grown canopies, allowing farming families to increase their incomes. Across the world, more than 18 million hectares of land have been restored using FMNR. And the story is not over yet: Tony hopes to see a billion hectares regenerated worldwide. What would this mean for the planet? A billion regenerated hectares could remove up to a quarter of the carbon in the earth's atmosphere. As climate change threatens, the stakes couldn't be much higher than that.

FMNR may not look like 'missionary work' as it is traditionally conceived, but Tony expands the definition of 'mission'. 'This is all God's work,' he says. 'God is actively involved in the restoration of creation.' FMNR first took root in Niger in West Africa, where Tony served as a missionary with his wife Liz (and, later, four children) for 17 years. They met at university before skipping across the pond to do a one year intensive 'Bible in Missions' course at the Bible College of New Zealand.

Tony is the first to admit he is not a natural student, and found it hard to sit in class while the mission field beckoned. While he appreciated the lectures and the readings, and looks back fondly on his teachers, at the time 'I was champing at the bit to get away!'

He found inspiration in personal stories, testimonies given by those who had worked as missionaries and returned. 'What spoke deeply to me,' says Tony, 'was people sharing their missionary experiences and how they lived out their faith.'

For Tony, faith has always been a part of life. Every night as a child, his Roman Catholic mother would pray with her six children before they went to bed. 'There was never the question, is there a God? Or is Jesus our saviour?' Tony says. As a teenager, his Catholic school ran a retreat on the Mornington Peninsula, which he wrote about many years later in his book, *The Forest Underground*: 'The camp director explained how we put on masks and try to be somebody we are not in order to be accepted. But because God loves us and accepts us just as we are, we do not need the approval of others.' This was a revelation for someone who had never been particularly confident. 'Feeling self-conscious, feeling inadequate, always trying to emulate someone else – the priest said this actually doesn't matter,' Tony says today. 'Jesus loves you just the way you are. I never had a road to Damascus experience, but this was a deepening of my faith.' At university, he was given a Bible in a readable translation. Never caring much about denominational labels, he moved across from the Catholic to the Evangelical tradition. By the time he got to Bible College Tony was growing in his biblical faith and knowledge.

Reading the Bible at home is one thing; reading it when you arrive as a missionary in a new country facing many challenges and where you don't speak the language or understand the culture is entirely another. 'It makes it much more real,' Tony says. 'Every day forces you onto your knees to say, God, what have I gotten myself into? Help me!'

Today, Tony is struck by how different it is to live, as he now does, back in the developed world. 'In some ways,' he says, 'despite the difficulties we had, I yearn for the times when I was forced to trust God every day. Back home I've got a good job, a regular salary, a good car – everything's laid on. Over there nothing was guaranteed. You were forced to rely on God.' Relying on God meant constantly returning to the scriptures and persisting in prayer. 'In reading God's word I found constant reassurance that God was in control, and that God answers prayer,' says Tony. 'The power of answered prayer in desperate situations had a profound effect on me.'

Relying on God came to mean something else as well: it meant trusting in the way God works through God's creation. This was a lesson learned the hard way. As an agronomist struggling in the barren landscapes of Niger, Tony at first did what seems the obvious thing to do if you want to re-green a desert: he planted trees. Huge efforts were put in to getting seedlings into the ground, only to see them fail to take hold. The discouragement was immense. But Tony continued to pray, to read the Bible – until, one day, a breakthrough came.

Tony has told the story many times. He was standing in a denuded landscape, his car parked by the side of the road, looking at dry, bare ground for miles in every direction. As he puts it in *The Forest Underground*, 'the futility and hopelessness of it all weighed heavily on me. North, south, east, west; as far as I could see there were empty, windswept plains. Even if I had hundreds of staff, a multimillion-dollar budget and many years to do the work, using the methods I was currently using, I would never make a significant or lasting impact.' In this moment of despair he glimpsed a small bush on the side of the road. 'Combing my hand through the foliage,' he writes, 'I let the leaves slide between my fingers.' He suddenly realised: 'This was not a bush. These leaves belonged to a tree. It had been cut down, and I was looking at shoots from a stump. I was standing,' Tony writes, 'on a subterranean forest.'

In a flash he realised that rather than planting exotic trees (remember the pine forests he played in as a child) he could help the trees that were already there to return. Before long, he had convinced around ten local farmers to give it a try. Many were sceptical at first, thinking their livelihoods depended on removing the bushes and tree stumps that dotted their land, not tending them. But eventually the benefits of each regenerated patch of land could be seen. Farmers looked to their neighbours' success and agreed to try it on their own land. In a recent paper, Tony wrote that 'from 1984, FMNR spread largely from farmer to farmer at an estimated rate of 250 thousand hectares per year for the next twenty years. On-farm tree density increased from four trees per hectare to forty, resulting in some 200 million trees restored across five million hectares of degraded land without planting a single tree.'

The story of Tony's insight in the desert is more than a scientific breakthrough; it is something like a parable. Jesus told stories to show the nature of God. Tony's story, repeated many times to audiences around the world, does the same thing. 'Nature's ability to heal is like God's willingness to forgive us,' he says. We can do all sorts of things to nature – burn it, cut it down, pollute it – but when we, in a sense, 'repent' of our destructive ways and work with nature instead of destroying it – it freely 'forgives us, comes back and blesses us in many ways.' In this way, says Tony, 'God's character is revealed through his creation. God is not just in the business of saving people, of healing broken lives; God is actively engaged in the restoration of his creation.'

This theological insight can transform the way we think about the environmental challenges we face. Rather than working *on* nature, we can work *with* it; and in so doing cooperate with the work of God. Tony notes that this is in contrast with some prevailing attitudes in the developed world. 'The scientific mind,' he says, 'has treated desertification as a technical issue. As long as we have enough money and resources and technology, we can reverse it. One of the surprises of the work I did in Africa is the power of God's creation to heal itself. Once you remove the constraints, the destruction and disrespect for nature, God has built into creation the capacity to self heal.'

There is a further lesson. Environmental challenges such as climate change seem insurmountable. Scientists and policymakers are scrambling for a solution. Tony thinks we should think a bit differently. 'Our Western mindset says: we have broken it, now we have to fix it. And we expect the solution to come from the West. Our money, our knowledge, our skills. But the champions of the Niger story are the poorest, most risk-averse, and often most illiterate people in the world. This is their story. They saw it was to their benefit to work with nature, rather than fighting against it and destroying it. They applied this to their land, and their neighbours copied them, and their neighbours' neighbours. How many programs,' Tony asks, 'deliberately go to the poor, the illiterate, the risk-averse, and ask them what to do, and expect them to lead change? How many with authority and power today seek solutions to climate change amongst those impacted the most by it?'

Can those of us living in the West learn to see ourselves as followers rather than leaders in the effort to combat climate change? This would require a big change in our self-understanding. To put in theological language, it would require a conversion, a conversion that can be helped by contact with those in the developing world. For all the good he did in his mission work, Tony says, 'the person most changed by our time in Africa was me.'

'You think you're going there to help people,' he explains. 'And you find that, yes, people are needy, people are poor. But they're generous. We in the West are quite possessive and often selfish. I learned by asking lots of questions and respecting the knowledge they had. You have to learn that you don't have all the answers. You have to be prepared to ask questions, to observe. And be humble enough to ask for help when you're wrong.'

Over many years, Tony has developed his approach to communities interested in trying FMNR. He comes with a respectful, open attitude. 'I don't accuse people of destroying God's creation!' he says. Instead, 'I ask questions. I ask: what was the environment like in your childhood, or in your parents' time? Almost universally, they describe the garden of Eden. The weather was regular and consistent. The soil was fertile. We had a secure supply of water. Women didn't have to go far to collect fuel. There were wild animals. Then I ask: what's it like today? And they describe the opposite. We can't grow enough food to see us through to the next harvest. Women have to walk for hours every day to collect fuel. Then I ask: if you continue with business as usual, destroying the environment, what will life be like for your children? Their response is – Tony, it will be hell on earth. We will have to leave our ancestral lands and go to the capital city. We will have to leave everything we know and love. Then I say: will you come on a journey with me? I think this will work. Let's try it on a small portion of your land, and we'll learn from each other the best way to proceed.

The journey has been a long one for Tony Rinaudo, but it's not over yet. A billion hectares of FMNR is a big ask – and not something he can do own his own, or even with the organisation he works for now, World Vision. Many partners will be involved, starting in Ethiopia, Kenya, Uganda and Zambia, and then right around the world. Tony's job now, he says, is less about working on the ground, and more about encouraging a change in mindset: '90 per cent of my work now is not technical at all. I'm not regreening landscapes, I'm regreening mindscapes. The battle is against false beliefs and negative attitudes. For example: that trees on farmland are weeds that need to be eliminated. I'm in the business of turning enemies of trees into friends of trees.'

False beliefs don't just exist in the mission field, but in the church at home as well. Here Tony sees great potential. 'The church is such a powerful, far reaching organisation. If we could understand the biblical mandate to be stewards of God's creation, we could change the world.' And yet, as Tony has written: 'Not only are we all too often silent about the deliberate and both random and systematic destruction of God's wonderful creation, for most of us our lifestyle, our profligate waste and toxic pollution, and our investments often support its destruction. Why is it so rare to hear words of righteous anger at the destruction of God's creation coming from our pulpits?'

What is his answer to this question? Sometimes, he thinks, there is a wariness in church circles, particularly within Evangelicalism, to fully embrace environmental causes. There is a fear of liberalism, of 'watering down the Gospel'. Tony thinks this is a big mistake. In a recent paper, he laid out four reasons why Christians should care for creation. First, he says, because creation belongs to God and is important to him. Second, because 'knowing that environmental destruction leads to human suffering, we care for creation as an act of love towards our neighbour.' Third, we care for creation because it is intrinsically good – the creation stories in Genesis make this clear. And the fourth reason why Christians should care for creation is perhaps the most interesting of all: 'This may be contentious,' Tony admits, 'but we should care for creation because the earth, albeit a renewed earth, will be our home for eternity.'

'When I was at university,' he explains, 'the preaching was that the earth is going to be burned up and we'll all be taken to heaven. This just didn't add up to me. Why would God go to such trouble to create such beauty and intricacy, just to burn it up?' For Tony, caring for creation is caring for our eternal home.

The hope of a restored creation inspires him to keep going. Tony sums up his idea of hope in the famous quotation sometimes attributed to St Augustine: 'Hope has two beautiful daughters. Their names are anger and courage; anger at the way things are, and courage to see that they do not remain the way they are.' 'Many young people today,' Tony observes, 'are discouraged and despairing the way I was when I was younger. I thought adults didn't care and that I couldn't change anything. But hope doesn't fall out of the sky and bless a selected few. Hope comes from action. We can make hope happen by tackling the things we're not happy with.'

By doing this himself, Tony has helped whole communities find hope. 'The biggest change in the places I've worked is the restoration of hope. When people have tried and failed so many times, it's hard to convince them to try again. They don't want to be disappointed. But when you go to those places today, it's like a picture of heaven: shouting, clapping, singing. It's within their means to create the future they want.'

FURTHER READING

Tony Rinaudo, *The Forest Underground: Hope for a Planet in Crisis*, ISCAST, 2022

Tony Rinaudo, 'Partnership with God in Restoring Creation: a Story of Hope' in *Missional Responses to Environmental and Human Calamities*, William Carey Publishing, 2024, ch. 14.

SEAN LAU

Sean Lau studied theology at Oxford University as a Rhodes Scholar, where he completed his doctoral thesis on 'The Relationship between Theology and Ethics in Modern Christian Thought.' He later studied law at Harvard Law School. Sean served as an associate at the High Court of Australia, and from 2014 to 2015 worked as a legal officer for the Honourable Peter McClellan, Chair of the Royal Commission into Institutional Responses to Child Sexual Abuse. Sean has practised as a solicitor at the Crown Solicitor's Office of New South Wales, and currently works at a US law firm.

'STRONG BUT BRITTLE' is how Sean Lau describes his Christian faith as a teenager. Growing up in Sydney, his parents having immigrated from Malaysia a few years before he was born, Sean came to faith in high school. 'The immigrant background matters,' he says today. 'I grew up as an Asian Australian in the 1990s and 2000s. I always felt a little out of place, like there wasn't ground under my feet – not quite Asian, not quite Australian. People around me struggled with the same thing.' It informed his spiritual journey: 'One of the things that attracted me to evangelicals was the absolute certainty with which they believed.'

Sean Lau is a former Rhodes Scholar with a doctorate in theology who now practises law in the United States. He attends an Anglican church in New York, though one somewhat removed from the Anglican churches he grew up around. Sydney Anglicans are known for a deep commitment to a particular kind of reformed and evangelical theology. As a teenager, Sean attended a conference in which a prominent Sydney Anglican leader proclaimed that John Calvin, the sixteenth-century Swiss church reformer, got Christian theology – and by extension, everything else – 99 per cent right. 'There was something comforting in that certainty,' Sean says today. Comforting, that is, until a series of personal and familial crises struck in his last years of high school. It was then he realised that the 'strong but brittle' faith he had acquired as a young teenager 'wasn't giving me the answers I needed to understand what I was going through.'

Many would have walked away. 'A lot of evangelicals,' says Sean, 'when they reach their crisis of faith, find they have questions about what they believe and that their Christian communities won't give them answers. So, they decide that their faith belonged to their childhood and now it's time to move on. I think I was unusual because I stumbled on a different part of the Christian theological tradition, one that evangelicals don't encounter often and are suspicious of when they do.'

This was Karl Barth – one of the most profound and influential theologians of the twentieth century. Barth is known for his insistence on the glory of God, on God's 'otherness', and on the inability of humans to approach God in their own strength and with their own resources. He is also known for writing and signing the 1934 *Barman Declaration*, a protest by Christians living in Germany who opposed the Nazis. One of Barth's co-signers – Dietrich Bonhoeffer – was arrested and executed for his opposition. Barth managed to make a new life in his native Switzerland.

Barth is a difficult writer, particularly for a young person not yet out of high school. 'You can imagine me at 16,' Sean says, 'puzzling through Barth's commentary on Romans, with obscure references to thinkers like Kierkegaard and Overbeck. But something captured me.' What stood out? 'The way Barth talks about the absolute reality of God. The evangelicalism I'd swum in focused on apologetics: here is all the historical evidence, here are all the arguments, here's why believing in God is only rational. But Barth, a few pages in, says that Christian apologetics is meaningless – that it reflects a secret psychological anxiety about your faith.'

For Barth, we can't reason ourselves or others into faith; nor can we learn about God by dutifully studying the world God has created. God is absolute and God's glory is beyond anything we can possibly conceive or understand. This might seem to distance us from the divine, but for Sean it was where he 'encountered God for the first time. It was confusing and hard to process. But it stirred the need I felt to study theology.'

That need would have to wait. As an undergraduate student, Sean studied law, and worked after graduating for a High Court Judge in Canberra. Afterwards, he received a job offer to work for Justice Peter McClellan, Chair of the recently established Royal Commission into Institutional Responses to Child Sexual Abuse. This was at the height – or perhaps the depth – of the scandal engulfing the churches, who were finally being called to account for the abuses against children that they had allowed, or turned a blind eye to, for decades.

'What attracted me to the role,' says Sean, 'was that Justice McClellan said he believed the Royal Commission would lead to lasting change for the Anglican and Catholic Churches.' Sean, like so many other Australian Christians, knew things needed to change. 'I came to the Commission hoping to help nudge the Church in a positive direction.'

Sean watched church leaders scramble to explain their failures to take action. 'I was struck by the sameness of the responses,' he says, 'across religions and across denominations. Theological differences didn't seem to play a role. There was always the denial of responsibility. The desire to protect the reputation of the organisation. The belief that a scandal would detract from the mission, so it had better be kept hidden. The gap in knowledge about good policies and practices.' He recalled one famous Pentecostal pastor called for examination. 'He was asked if he knew what a conflict of interest in decision-making was, and his answer was that he felt conflicted over his hard choices.' Were examples like this theology gone wrong or simply theology ignored? 'Sometimes there was a theological veneer attached to the responses,' says Sean. 'For example, some Catholic leaders might talk about stewarding the church's resources, and argue that paying out abuse survivors wasn't good stewardship. I'm still not sure how much of this theology was *ex post facto* – after the fact – brought in to justify what churches had already decided to do.'

Where theology was brought in it was often used badly. Sean singles out the concept of forgiveness. 'One less helpful way "forgiveness" was used was when churches pressured survivors to forgive their perpetrators. Or when churches said "we forgive the perpetrators" – and put them straight back into ministry. These were times when theology was doing work but in unhelpful ways.'

Did working at the Royal Commission change Sean's view of the church, or of theology? 'I was disillusioned by churches' abilities to address complex ethical problems. Church leaders had robust theologies at the level of theory. They knew what they believed. But when they were faced with this unspeakable situation that they had never dealt with before – serious and credible allegations of child sexual abuse within their ranks – they panicked. They fell back on platitudes, such as "let's do what our lawyers tell us to do" or "let's do nothing and hope it blows over".'

Not long after his work on the Royal Commission, Sean won a Rhodes Scholarship to study at Oxford. As a brilliant law student and promising young lawyer, many would have expected him to study law. He chose theology instead, attending seminars on Augustine, Martin Luther, and Bonhoeffer. 'Oxford was the first time,' he says, 'when I could put down my legal glasses and concentrate on the big-picture questions I wanted to work through. It was probably the most intellectually stimulating experience of my life, having the space and time to read and pursue what I wanted.' So his experiences at the Royal Commission hadn't turned him off the church entirely? No, says Sean. 'It made me more curious. It made me think about the relationship between theology and ethics. When I first proposed a doctoral dissertation at Oxford, I said I wanted to study how theology related to cases of child abuse, and the issue of forgiveness.'

The opportunity to read widely challenged some of the new certainties Sean had adopted to replace his old certainties. 'I was still enamoured by Barth when I arrived at Oxford,' he admits. 'I once joked to my supervisor that, when I'm not certain about something, I go to Barth, and he probably got it right.' This was an obvious echo of what Sean had heard said about Calvin in Sydney all those years ago. But: 'When I immersed myself in theology, one thing I found was the sheer diversity of the subject; that almost every position that some Christians have defended – maybe literally to the death – has been contested by other Christians. The more you know about church history, the more you realise how provisional most theological judgments are.'

For his thesis, Sean eventually decided not to look at the child abuse crisis alone, but at the relationship between theology and ethics more broadly. 'Twentieth-century theologians treated that relationship as a way to work through how theology should relate to real life,' he explains. 'And they had very different ideas based on their priorities. For some theologians, the concern was to say, even once you've worked out your theological theory, there's a practical and entirely distinct question about what to do next. Others, like liberation theologians working out of Latin America, had observed intense experiences of poverty and human misery as pastors. They were frustrated that other theologians, who often came from a place of privilege, kept talking about "ethics" but had nothing to say about those experiences. And other theologians, like Barth and Bonhoeffer, wanted to stop confusion between what a majority-Christian culture says about God and what God is actually saying.' Sean's thesis identified these competing approaches to thinking about theology and ethics, and argued that each attempted to capture a particular aspect of what it means to live a Christian life. 'What I concluded,' says Sean, 'was that as different as the approaches were, one thing they had in common was an attempt to grapple with theology's limits in making sense of Christian life. Theology can't tell you how to make practical decisions and it can't explain the experiences that shape your life; it can't even substitute for what God is telling you.' And there was a personal realisation too: 'Being a Christian and studying theology doesn't mean knowing how my own life story will shake out. My story is going to be messy.'

This messiness was an antidote to the 'strong but brittle' faith of Sean's younger years. He describes his thesis as, among other things, 'an attempt to bring intellectual humility to theology.' The messiness he found was not only in opposition to the certainty of some Sydney Anglicans, but it also helped Sean to 'attempt to argue against a number of Christian theologians who try to make theology do too much.'

'At the Royal Commission I felt disillusioned over the state of Christian churches, and at Oxford I became disillusioned over the state of theology today,' he says. 'Theology is not in a good way right now, even if I'm still committed to the enterprise.' How so? 'Theologians want to be relevant. They want to make theology do stuff, change people's behaviour, make sense of messy situations. That comes from a place of anxiety. In medieval and early modern Europe, theologians called the shots; Calvin ran Geneva. But now the university and rest of society ignore them. So theologians compensate by arguing that theology solves everything.' What's an example of this? 'One of my old supervisors, John Milbank, says that if you get Christian theology right then you don't need sociology; theology becomes its own social science. Whereas I tried to argue in my doctoral thesis that theology should have a more modest role.'

His aspirations for a 'modest' theology come in part from working in law. 'Lawyers are trained not to overgeneralise,' he says. 'Every case turns on its own facts. Ideas still matter, and I studied theology to understand how it could inform both legal practice and real-life concerns. But some theologians oversell what their ideas can achieve. I think of one theologian who suggests we can solve child abuse by buying into her doctrine of the Trinity.' Sean admits he is oversimplifying. 'But when I first encountered that way of thinking while working at the Royal Commission, I thought, that doesn't seem especially practical! You need to speak to the actual survivors; the mental health or social workers who grapple with this every day; the lawyers litigating cases.'

So what *should* be the role of theology? 'Theology is often best when it's a stop sign,' Sean proposes. 'When it says: "Look, you think you're speaking in the name of God. Actually, you're not. Why not take a breather and think about what God really wants?"' Sean points to some issues that divide Christians. 'When I was growing up in the Sydney Anglican church, the issue of the day was whether women could preach in church. But whatever your stance, there's still the meta-question of why you care so much about the issue, because today's issue may not be tomorrow's. Christians once ripped out each other's tongues for what they said about Christ's two wills; nowadays almost no one understands those debates. So why is women preaching what you've decided to fall on your sword for?'

Sean sees the disruptive potential of theology as a good thing. 'Luther used to say that sin is being turned in on yourself, like an ingrown toenail, but divine grace opens us up both to God and the world. One reason I remain Christian is because I'm still amazed by how God calls us out from ourselves. He disrupts our lives and challenges us. What we used to think was important, theologically or practically, might turn out not to matter, and God can completely reorient us. I worry that more dogmatic forms of Christianity have lost that openness to God.' He adds: 'That's what I would want to make sure is preserved in theological education, too.'

Given all this, what's next? Sean has found himself in the United States, resuming legal practice after some further study at Harvard Law School. 'America is a big and diverse place', he says. 'It has a rich even if ambiguous history. People have thought long and hard about theories of social change and how to put ideas into practice.' Currently, Sean is an attorney at a New York law firm. Religion remains important to his work: he has represented clients, including a coalition of minority religious groups, in religious freedom and church-state litigation.

And personally? How has his theological journey changed the way he thinks about faith? First: 'I enjoy stories that go deep into theology but end with a character being sent out into the world to do something useful.' Sean laughs. 'I may be a bit biased! But I'm thinking of Dostoevsky's *Brothers Karamazov*, or Marilynne Robinson's *Gilead*.' And second: 'I get a lot of comfort from the biblical wisdom books. The evangelical tradition I grew up in assumed that life is a straight line from Point A to Point B, a vocation God sets in stone for you. But Hebrew wisdom paints life as more episodic, a loosely connected set of vignettes. David Kelsey wrote a theological anthropology that's good on this. The idea is that there isn't always a thread weaving your life together. If there is, that's up to God, and the thread won't be visible to you. That definitely helped me during the pandemic, when life was as chaotic as it was. So even though I don't exactly know where I'm going, I still hope to serve God.'

What might that look like? 'I worry a lot about Christian nationalism and the harm it causes, both to people and to Christian faith. Look at the way the rhetoric of Australia as a Christian nation gets used to justify the horrendous treatment of refugees. On the flip side, cosiness by Christians with political power and cultural acceptance doesn't protect Christian faith. It usually corrupts it.'

Sean won't be drawn into where he sees himself in five years' time. 'There's been too much disruption over the last few years to make plans,' he says. 'In my defence, Bonhoeffer has this essay where he says that the world may not be stable enough for planning to make sense. So you need to live each day both responsibly and like it's your last. But maybe I'm too much of a millennial and that's just me giving into the social and cultural milieu.' Maybe – or maybe it's a manifestation of a new 'theology of messiness.' But even if he can't tell us exactly what he'll be doing, 'I can tell you what kind of person I would hope to be. I'm still Christian. My faith and my theology have become more complex. I would like to be a person who is still faithful to God and someone who is able to love others – hopefully in a wiser and more nuanced way than when I was younger. I'm not sure if I can say more than that.' That's saying quite a lot. Any plans to return to Australia? 'Maybe! But I'm leaving that up to God. The world is a very complicated place. I'm willing to see where life takes me.'

FURTHER READING

Sean Lau, 'The Distinction between Theology and Ethics: A Critical History,' *Journal of Religious Ethics*, 52(2), 209-230 (2024).

Julie Edwards

Julie Edwards is CEO of Jesuit Social Services. She has over 40 years' experience engaging with marginalised people and families experiencing breakdown and trauma. She is a social worker, family therapist, and a grief and loss counsellor. Julie has a Masters in Social Work and has completed a PhD in organisational identity. She has served on a number of government and philanthropic committees and is a member of the International Working Group on Death, Dying and Bereavement. Julie is a member of a number of national and international Jesuit commissions and working groups across areas of justice, education, social ministry and ecology.

THERE IS A STATUE of St Ignatius, the founder of the Jesuit order, which captures him in full stride, in a long flowing coat, one foot planted firmly on the ground with the other raised to propel him forward. As CEO of Jesuit Social Services, Julie Edwards has spoken often about this image. It suggests a readiness to move, to be where the need is, to be restless in pursuit of justice and peace. But the raised foot also speaks of 'the pause that exists before the foot is planted', she says: the need to take time to reflect on experience, on where we have been and on where we are going. This image says a lot about what Julie Edwards is trying to do at Jesuit Social Services, and it also says a lot about her.

Julie Edwards is both an activist and a contemplative. By profession a social worker and counsellor, for the last eighteen years she has led Jesuit Social Services, a 'social change organisation' working to build a just society. Active across Australia, Jesuit Social

Services works with people exiting prison with nowhere to go; people struggling with mental illness or substance use or both; people unable to find work due to discrimination. There is also a strong advocacy component. Jesuit Social Services stands with the poor and speaks to the powerful.

But throughout her time with the organisation – and indeed throughout her life – Julie Edwards has also recognised the importance of 'the pause before the foot is planted', and has nurtured this aspect of her life through retreats, meditation, journalling, and now a PhD. Each of these is a way of reflecting on her experiences and discerning the next step forward. Of course, in a Christian context, to reflect on experience is to do theology, even if it's not always given that name. When we met we asked Julie to tell us something about her faith background.

'My family's background is Irish Catholic,' she told us. 'I was part of a Catholic tribe – one of 38 cousins!' A religious upbringing? 'It wasn't particularly spiritual or religious; it was more about how you are with people.' Her parents set the tone: 'My mother was very kind and compassionate – always tuned into who was being left out of the conversation. Dad had very high ethical standards. He wouldn't have put the word social justice on it, but if he was in the phone box and twenty cents dropped down, he'd put it back. He was scrupulous about things like that.'

Julie was educated by the Brigidine Sisters, an Irish order of nuns named for the patroness of Ireland, St Brigid of Kildare. Their ethos affected the students, including Julie. 'They had the attitude that you don't take anything with you when you die. That you should be kind to the kid in the playground who is being left out, that sort of thing.' There was also an emphasis on the humanity and emotionality of Jesus. 'I remember Mother Gabriel telling us that Jesus wept at times. These things were marbled through the culture of the school.'

But with the end of school came the end of faith – or at least this particular expression of faith. 'I left school in 1972. By then, I was a feminist into Germaine Greer, Betty Friedan, people like that. I was very critical of the church. I thought it was sexist – which it is – and patriarchal – which it is. I actually got very flat, very depressed. I started doing yoga, which really helped me.'

She took up social work, which was then a relatively new profession. But before long she found herself itching to travel, and went to India. 'At the end of my second year at uni I thought, that's it, I'm out of here.' There was a certain irony in the particular place she ended up. 'There I was, a vegan macrobiotic yoga devotee, who had been so outspoken about the church, how it was completely irrelevant, how it was all crap, and I headed straight into the arms of Mother Teresa's Missionaries of Charity.'

On the streets of Calcutta, the Missionaries served (and still serve) the poorest of the poor. This was not poverty as Julie had seen it in Australia; this was overwhelming destitution, intense suffering, hunger, illness and death. The work of the Sisters in the midst of this reflected a side of Christianity that Julie had never actually rejected: 'What I love about Christianity is the practical, service side of it,' she says. 'The fact that it's centered on the most marginalised. I think the antecedents of my current faith were there in India. It was not about rediscovering my faith; I was discovering it for the first time.'

This focus on the most marginalised still operates in many parts of the church today. Julie gives an example: 'When Jesuit Social Services wanted to start a new school for marginalised young people, we tried to get the education department to fund it and we couldn't. I went to the Catholic Education Office and they said, "Of course we'll fund it." I nearly fell off my seat. They said, of course we will, that's who we are.'

Back home after her time in India, Julie began to explore the idea of Christian community. At the age of 21 she found herself living with two other women who were also devoted to radical faith and communal living. 'We only met properly the first night we moved in together!', Julie says. It was a steep learning curve. 'We had to find ways to connect. We had no shared views about anything. At first, we experimented with having some quiet time together. Then as we evolved, we basically became more monastic than the Catholics – we prayed the office, chanted, had silent prayer before and after.' Ancient habits came naturally to people who had come together to serve the poor.

Serving the marginalised in community brought the Christian faith alive for Julie. 'Two things came out of it for me. One was about people on the margins: living in community and serving the marginalised taught me what the crucifixion meant, what the resurrection meant. And the other is about how we live as Christians. Is faith something we do on Sundays, with maybe a bit of volunteering on Wednesday nights? Or is it about where we get our food, where our clothes come from, who we live with, who our friends are? These are the questions that emerged for me from that heady, intense time.'

Flash forward to today. Heading Jesuit Social Services is, in some ways, a far cry from working one on one with those in poverty on the streets of India, or living in a tiny intentional community serving the most disadvantaged people in Melbourne – but in other ways it's not that far at all. One of the most striking things about Julie's work at Jesuit Social Services, and about her reflections on that work in her PhD thesis, is the way she has tried to bring the ethos that fuelled those early, radical Christian experiences to what is now a large, national organisation, with many employees, many of whom have no explicit Christian commitment at all.

Being on the side of the marginalised has meant opposing, for example, the 'neoliberal' trends she has seen encroaching on the social welfare sector. 'The neoliberal frame,' says Julie, 'is about value for money. It's about the economic contribution people can make. I'm very happy for people to be supported to get back to work, but for me it's not so that they contribute economically, or stop taking welfare. It's about their wanting to belong and to contribute to society more broadly.'

Julie is not the first to have questioned whether an emphasis on economic efficiency and individual freedom can undermine communities and leave vulnerable people behind, but she is in a unique position to see its effects. 'Ultimately,' she says, 'it comes down to the question, how are people who are poor seen? In the neoliberal frame, people are seen as consumers or users of services or clients. At Jesuit Social Services, I don't talk about clients, I talk about *participants*.' And language is important. 'It's about giving people a sense of agency, a sense that they have something to contribute. It's about belonging and connectedness.'

Pushing back against prevailing government attitudes can make it harder to survive as an organisation. 'There's a big push to squeeze our work into certain frameworks,' says Julie. 'The system tends to favour big organisations who can take things to scale.' Despite this official preference for the large and scaleable, Jesuit Social Services has had remarkable success over the years in serving those who are often forgotten and sometimes despised – people exiting prison being an obvious example. What does treating people as participants rather than clients look like on the ground? 'It's about how we talk to people, the dignity we affirm in people,' Julie says. 'Particular programs lend themselves to that: our Support After Suicide program, for example, where people who have lost someone to suicide are brought to a critical point where they're wrestling with a lot of things. Or picking up a person from prison.' These small acts – the ways in which we respond to people, our demeanour, the time we take – are things that can't be measured. They don't appear in government statistics. And yet they are some of the most important aspects of Jesuit Social Services' work.

We asked Julie what difference being a Jesuit organisation makes. Is there a spiritual aspect to the work? 'Given the view I have of the human being,' she says, 'I want us to be able to attend to people's deepest desires. I don't go along with Maslow's hierarchy, you know, the idea that once you've met your basic needs, then you can think about your spiritual needs. Poor people all around the world think about spiritual things.' But how can you incorporate serving these other, more spiritual, needs in the secular environment we live in? 'This is a question for us as an organisation,' she replies. 'It's not about proselytising, which I hate. It's about helping people to be reflective. As a Jesuit once said to me: the Holy Spirit can do the rest. It's about opening up spaces for people to reflect on who they are and what they want.' This is a difficult tension and many Christian organisations are wrestling with it. 'That's what I was trying to do in my PhD thesis,' says Julie. 'Navigate that space.'

Julie has reflected more deeply than most on the question of how to maintain a traditional religious ethos and identity in an organisation that, by its very nature, exists in a secular context. Her PhD is in an area of sociology called 'organisational identity'. It is about – in Julie's words – 'the current challenge for the Jesuits to fulfil their mission and ensure that organisations bearing their name operate with a distinct and meaningful identity as their numbers diminish and as these organisations are increasingly staffed and led by laypeople.' So how can this be done? That would (and did) take 80,000 words to explain. But Julie emphasises one thing: 'I think we need to let go of some of our language, some of our symbols which have become hurdles for people.'

'I love Christianity but I'm very disappointed with many dominant forms of it. It's clear others are too – they're fleeing elsewhere to get what they need, like to Buddhism, yoga, meditation. The Church often just appears too interested in its brand.' What can be done about this? One thing she feels is missing from current Christian spirituality is the body – a recognition of the fact that we are physical beings. 'I've done yoga on and off for years,' she says, 'and I've recently begun doing Tai Chi. I wish that Christianity – which is supposed to be an incarnational religion – had more embodied practices. We kneel and bow and all that, but it's very strange that we don't use our bodies much.' Julie is also disappointed that there is not a stronger focus on developing our capacity for contemplation. But there's hope: 'I'm glad to hear Catholic schools are now teaching meditation to really little kids. It's a practical tool for life.'

Julie follows other spiritual practices too. 'In my 20s and 30s I tried to make an eight day retreat every year,' she says. 'I've done that sort of thing on and off. But then in my 50s, around the time I was made CEO of Jesuit Social Services, I'd be sitting here looking out the window, looking at the clouds when I was supposed to be reading the business continuity plan in front of me. I'd be thinking, maybe I'm just the wrong person for this job.' This forced a new kind of spiritual focus. 'It had to do with menopause, too,' she says. 'It's a bit like when you're pregnant: there's an inner life happening in you and you're carrying around this secret. It's quite a spiritual time. Menopause was like that. This is when I started a more regular practice of half an hour or an hour's silent time every day. And I basically never miss that.'

And what do you find when you do this? 'I'm not someone who goes around having mystical experiences all the time,' says Julie, 'but occasionally when I've been on retreat or been quiet, I've had moments when I have a sense of God. It's like you can feel the leaves on the trees around you and the person you're dealing with and there is a oneness.' It's not hard to see how this way of seeing the world can inform the work of an organisation like Jesuit Social Services. 'In the last ten years or so,' says Julie, 'my thinking has crystallised around the word "interconnectedness". It's a word I still use a lot. We're actually all one. We are inherently relational: even my body is a series of cells, and that's relational too. It's just how things are. It's a different understanding from saying, "be kind to this person," or even, "I can learn from that person." We're *actually* one. God, the universe – whatever is at the heart of everything – is love, and we're all connected. So this poor person I'm serving and I are just the one thing, rather than their being someone out there whom I am called to help. We're all inherently the same.'

There are some lessons here for theological institutions, too. These should be in the business, according to Julie, of 'creating opportunities to see that interconnectedness.' And they should not neglect the fact that we are physical beings. 'This leads to thinking about where you put your body. How do you make room for that insight about interconnectedness to emerge? How do I see my false perceptions, keep taking those layers off?' We come back to talking about the founder of the Jesuits. 'Ignatius had his leg smashed in a war,' says Julie. 'He was convalescing, and he had nine months stuck in bed to reflect, to have a look at his own life.' She suggests we all need to confront ourselves in this honest way. 'Let's take the scales off our eyes and really look at our reality.' Ultimately, she says, 'theology should be about how you live.'

How much have Julie's views evolved since she first served the poor in radical Christian communities in Melbourne? 'My approach has developed,' she says. 'But it's not that different, in a way. It's just that once my focus would have been more on the person of Jesus, seeing Jesus in the poor, whereas now I see God as marbled through everything. The question is, are we in that flow?

Are we in the flow of God's love, building and strengthening and healing relationships? Or are we somewhere else?'

Julie's vision is a hopeful one, despite the challenges of working amongst poverty and disadvantage. Where does hope come from? 'If I believe that God is love,' she says, 'and that all that exists is sort of like an explosion of God's love, and God is through it, and we're all interconnected, and it's all held in love, and I have just a small part to play in that – then that's my basis for hope. Ultimately, we might ruin this whole planet, but actually God continues. God is much bigger than all that and will hold everything. This doesn't mean we should just give up and do nothing. But it means we should do what we're doing in the context of this faith which is all about love. Love as the deepest driver, propelling everything and holding everything together. It's actually a story of hope.'

Further reading

Julie Edwards, 'Fostering Organisational Identity in a Community Service Organisation: A Jesuit Approach' (PhD Thesis), La Trobe University, Department of Social Work and Social Policy, 2021

Julie Edwards, 'Incarceration in a changing climate', in *Eureka Street*, 18 January 2022 (online)

Stan Grant

Stan Grant is a Wiradjuri and Kamilaroi man. He has worked as a journalist for the ABC, SBS, the Seven Network and Sky News Australia. From 2001 to 2012, he worked for CNN as an anchor and senior correspondent in Asia and the Middle East. He has received a string of prestigious international and Australian awards for his journalism. In 2015, he published his bestselling book Talking to My Country, *which won the Walkley Book Award, and he also won a Walkley Award for his coverage of Indigenous affairs. In 2016, he was appointed to the Referendum Council on Indigenous Recognition. Stan was Professor of Global Affairs at Griffith University and is currently Vice-Chancellor's Chair of Australian-Indigenous Belonging at Charles Sturt University. His latest book is* The Queen Is Dead: Time for a Public Reckoning *(Harper Collins).*

AS A BOY, Stan Grant stood in the little shack where his grandmother lived, and looked through to a bedroom where his uncles were kneeling in prayer. This sight, and the feeling that went with it, never left him. 'The room shook,' he says, 'with the force of God. You could feel it – I felt it. I felt it very personally. I felt God within me.' He adds: 'I've always wrestled with that.'

When he hosted *Q+A* on the ABC, Stan opened each show in the language of his people, the Wiradjuri people from what is now known as central New South Wales. This was not something we had seen on mainstream Australian television before, and it speaks of the importance of language in Stan's thinking about the world.

'In Wiradjuri, we have a saying,' he says, 'which means "no language, no people".' For generations, white people did everything they could to get rid of the Wiradjuri language. Stan's great-grandfather was arrested for speaking it on the streets of his home town. His father – also called Stan Grant – was behind a massive project at Charles Sturt University to save the Wiradjuri language for generations to come. He taught the younger Stan that 'language is not *who* you are, it is *where* you are.' That is, language is tied, not first and foremost to personal identity, but to place.

'This is a fundamental philosophical shift from the Western worldview,' says Stan. 'The Western idea of modernity arose out of the idea of *who* you are: all of the things that connect us to a sense of place and belonging were supplanted by the idea of the individual, and the individual as sovereign.' Hand in hand with modernity and individualism went empire, which is also closely connected with language, the denial of language – and place.

'One of the tools of empire is to silence people,' Stan says. 'It happened in the first British colony in Ireland, where they took away the ability of people to speak in their own language. When the British invaded Australia, we saw it in full force: silencing language, destroying culture, taking away our place in the world. We ceased to be Wiradjuri people or Kamilaroi people or Dharawal people. We ceased to be Gadigal people or Wurundjeri people, and we became "Aboriginal" people. "Indigenous" people. We lost our place in the world. Language is a way of claiming that back, of speaking from where we are, and of inviting Australians, too, to see their place in the country where they are, rather than just focusing on who they are.'

Stan Grant has been a journalist for more than 30 years, first in Australia and then as a senior correspondent for CNN in Asia and the Middle East. More recently, he has written a regular column for the ABC, and he presented the current affairs discussion program

Q+A until in May 2023 he stepped back, citing the toll on himself and his family of the racist abuse he regularly receives. 'Racism is a crime,' he wrote in his final column on the ABC website. 'Racism is violence. And I have had enough.' He went on: 'I take time out because we have shown again that our [Aboriginal] history – our hard truth – is too big, too fragile, too precious for the media. The media sees only battle lines, not bridges. It sees only politics.'

It is a great loss. There are not many voices in the Australian media who can bring the three perspectives that Stan offers: a First Nations perspective; a global perspective acquired not just by reading about global affairs but from many years of reporting from the ground; and the perspective of a person of faith.

This last is particularly rare, but, for Stan, God has been a constant presence. In his faith community growing up, in the Aboriginal churches on the missions where his uncles were pastors and his aunts were elders, in the bedroom where his uncles knelt in prayer, the presence of God was taken for granted. 'We did not ask, does God exist?' Stan says. 'I don't think it is possible to ask that as a First Nations person – certainly not as a Wiradjuri person.'

Instead, they asked a different question: 'Where is God?' This was, and is, a piercing question for a people who carry a heavy history of suffering. 'I was born in the sixties,' Stan says, 'when the idea of assimilation had really taken root. The word that was used was for us to be "absorbed" into the Commonwealth. Children were taken away, cultures were lost.' In the midst of this, 'the books of the Bible that spoke most profoundly to us were the stories of exile, of exodus, the stories of suffering and affliction, of lamentation, the story of Job, the story of Christ on the cross: My God, my God, why have you forsaken me? I've often described this as the church of the forsaken. We *were* the afflicted.'

Theology looks very different in this context than in the predominately white churches where the powerful pray. Throughout his life, Stan has read philosophy and theology in order, he says, to 'find the language and the people who could guide me on that search to answer the question: why do these things happen? What is the place of God? How can God allow this? And how do we as people of God live with that affliction, and still find hope? Theology gave me a language to speak back to the horrors of the world that I'd experienced, that my people had gone through, and that I'd seen in my reporting as well.'

Stan's reporting has taken him to some harrowing places. He has stood among the rubble of bombed out cities. He has watched mothers searching for the remains of their children among the stones. He has interviewed both the victims of atrocities and their perpetrators. He has seen, in the faces of refugees and others struck down by war and poverty, echoes of the sufferings experienced by his own people. In his most recent book but one – *With the Falling of the Dusk* – he wrote: 'When I looked into the eyes of a child or a parent in a refugee camp, I saw the eyes of my own family.'

If theology is to mean anything in Australia in the twenty-first century, it must answer to this kind of experience. In the aftermath of the Second World War, under the deep shadow cast by the Holocaust, German theologians like Jürgen Moltmann and Johann Baptist Metz grappled with what Europe had been through and, devastatingly, what their own people had done. Stan Grant's doctoral work at Charles Sturt University draws on the work of those who wrote theology after Auschwitz, who wondered how they could speak back to the world through the words of Jesus Christ after the Nazi death camps. Stan considers the question posed by the contemporary theologian Miroslav Volf: 'Can I, as a Croatian, embrace a Serbian nationalist fighter, after all the horrible things that have been done?' Volf says no, he can't – and yet he must. In this tension, Stan finds the mystery of God.

It's not about finding resolution. Rather, it is about waiting on God in the midst of suffering. This is not, says Stan, a hopeless position. 'Simone Weil wrote that God withdraws from the world to allow us to live in it,' he says, 'and leaves the trace of love so we can find God.' He offers some examples of God withholding his presence from the world: 'It's Christ on the cross – the moment of feeling forsaken. It's Lamentations – the most poetic part of the Bible and perhaps the saddest thing ever written – which arrives at the point when all is lost, Jerusalem is sacked, the enemies have won, and mothers give birth to children just to eat them out of hunger. At that point, there is only the wait for God.' He explains the personal relevance of these stories: 'As someone whose family, whose people have suffered the worst, what do we do? For me it is in the waiting. Hope sits in the worst of the affliction. I don't look for resolution.'

Theology is done in the waiting. Stan reaches not only to the post-Auschwitz German theologians, and not only to other Christian sources, but first and foremost to a concept at the heart of his own culture: 'In Wiradjuri we have a word, "*yindyamarra*,"' Stan says. 'Some see it as a philosophy, a way of being. It's about respect. It's about kindness. It's about being quiet in the world. It's about truth. It's about grace and love and forgiveness. And it's long occurred to me that what we're talking about when we talk about *yindyamarra* is not a philosophy but a theology. It's a way of being able to answer the questions that I've grappled with all my life. Why would God allow these things to happen to us?' Stan's doctoral work brings the concept of *yindyamarra* together with the thought of other great figures such as Simone Weil and St John of the Cross. These are writers who found God in stillness; indeed, in darkness.

'To be stripped of your senses,' says Stan, 'to wait for God to be revealed to you, to wait for that truth that comes to the few who have suffered great affliction – I've connected that to *yindyamarra* as a way for me to be able to endure and survive. In Miroslav Volf's phrase: to take the worst of history and remember it rightly – not to forget it, not to rush to reconciliation, not to smooth over the evils of history – but to find a place to put it and remember it rightly, without vengeance and without the resentment that only fuels more violence. *Yindyamarra* is a philosophy and a theological idea and a practice that allows me to live with the worst that has happened to my people.'

By drawing on *yindyamarra* and Christian thinkers who wrestled with the presence of God in the darkest of times, Stan finds language that can speak to the experiences of First Nations people in Australia. Secular language won't do the job. The enlightenment effort to 'de-mythologise' the world, says Stan, has run its course. What went wrong? He recently told a group of scientists that 'if there is one difference between us – between my people and the scientists' world of science, of cold, hard, enlightenment rationality – is that they asked the question that our people never asked: Does God exist? That fundamental break,' says Stan, 'allows all hell to break loose. From the moment that question is asked you have set us on the road to the gulag and the gas chamber.'

This disengagement from God in the West sits at the heart of the malaise of modernity. 'So many younger people I see are lost,' Stan says. 'Every morning I go for a walk along the beach where I live. I see young people there before sunrise. They're not there just to see a nice sunrise and take a picture. There is a yearning. A void. The Western world leaves us untethered. It leaves us alienated. It strips the enchantment from the world. There is a yearning for the divine in our lives.'

How do we satisfy this yearning? How do we as a nation find the divine in our lives, and in our common life? Stan is blunt: 'I don't believe white Australians can come to God in this country unless they come through us, as God's people in the land that God gave us.'

Of course, he goes on, 'we come to God through God. God reveals God to us. It is in meditation, prayer, nature, opening yourself to God that God reveals himself to you. But how can we do that when we have failed to see First Nations people as God's people in the land God gave us? It says in the Bible very clearly that to blaspheme against the Son of Man is forgiven, but to blaspheme against God is not. Is there a greater blasphemy than looking at our people and not being able to see in us God's own creation? We are the image of God. To kill us in the frontier wars, to poison our rivers, to take our children, is to sin against God. To steal from us is to steal from God. There is a necessary atonement that needs to take place in this country.'

Atonement is a theological concept. But the discussion about reconciliation between Aboriginal and non-Aboriginal people in Australia is usually carried out in the political sphere. And this, says Stan, will not do what we want it to do. When we spoke, Australia was grappling with how to respond to the Uluru Statement from the Heart: a call from First Nations people for a Voice to the Australian Parliament, for a treaty with the Australian Government, and for a process of truth-telling about what has happened in the past.

'I see the Uluru Statement as a fundamentally spiritual offering,' Stan says. 'You can see the hand of God in it. But how quickly we've jumped from that to a discussion of the Voice to Parliament. The Voice is just a political representation of the greater aspirations and the spirituality that are at the heart of the Uluru Statement. I think the debate around the Voice has stripped so much of the sacred from the Uluru Statement from the Heart. It's taken a thing of God and made it a thing of Caesar. This is so often where we end up: our default position is a political discussion. I think we need a much deeper spiritual discussion to even begin that conversation.'

By entering into that deeper spiritual discussion, we can, thinks Stan, help Australians come to the divine in a new way. 'Australians would much rather put these questions in the political realm than the spiritual. But in the West the political answers are not landing. People are yearning for something, they don't know what. Add in the cynicism, the scepticism, the turn away from faith, and we see, you know, Botox and bad television, which are poor substitutes for the things of the soul!'

If politics won't get us there, nor will philosophy alone. 'Philosophy can take you to the water's edge,' says Stan, 'but it doesn't get into the water. There's no surrender in philosophy. There is just the idea of trying to bring God to earth and tame God, control God, explain everything, when sometimes you have to surrender to it, and find God in the surrender.'

How then can theology speak to the current moment? How can we talk about the things that are found in surrender, in the deeper waters of prayer and meditation and scripture? Stan admits it is difficult. In Australia, 'to talk openly about God, to talk about Jesus Christ, has people looking askance at you. We don't have the literacy in the media, it doesn't have a place in our daily debate, because it's supplanted by politics. Politics has captured a lot of religious discourse, and twisted it out of shape, and put it in the service, particularly, of the worst aspects of conservative politics. People who have a flimsy understanding of faith and the scriptures have twisted those words into political slogans. It's so rare that we hear theologians, serious-minded people, people with knowledge of the world and a vantage point to speak to the world, engaged in this discussion.'

A start would be to be unafraid of using theological language. 'I see people of faith pulling their punches,' Stan says. 'We need to be able to have the conversation in a no-holds-barred way, to use the language of race, of forgiveness, of God, to talk about lament, about being able to cry the tears of God for the terrible things that have been done. To use the language of affliction, suffering, forsakenness, abandonment. The language that was all around me when I was growing up.' Stan sees an opportunity to feed this language into the public discussion. 'There is a sense of righteous anger at the injustice Aboriginal people face,' he says. 'We can seize this moment and say, there's another way of looking at this. We can connect the dots between people's yearning, and a higher calling for justice and love and forgiveness and grace and kindness in our world.'

For his part, Stan is on the front foot. 'I've felt profoundly called to speak to this moment through these ideas because politics just doesn't do it. Politics is insufficient. Philosophy is insufficient. It is only theology that gives me the language and the clear air to grapple with questions that politics just cannot get close to. I feel that it is part of my duty as a Wiradjuri person to say: we offer you our forgiveness and love. The grace that comes from knowing who we are. The grace that comes from never having to ask: does God exist?'

Dare we hope that grace has the last word? Despite the pain associated with all that has happened in the past, and despite the mess of politics and division that we see in Australia today, Stan's latest book, *The Queen is Dead*, ends in a moment of grace. 'When the Queen died,' Stan explains, 'it was an incredibly confronting, challenging, cathartic moment for me in a way that I didn't anticipate. At the ABC everybody put on black suits. I felt betrayed and I felt abandoned. I said, I cannot put on black and mourn the passing of what the Queen represents. I wasn't talking about her as an individual, but what she represents, what's happened to my people – I said no, I can't square that.'

The book draws together this experience, this anger, along with the concept of *yindyamarra*, with reflections on the legacy of colonialism, and reflections on Australia at this point in our history – and on top of all of this, with a moment of grace: 'I was at my father's house one day,' Stan explains. 'I'd been down to the river, where I always find the spirit of my people. And I went for a run past a church. I heard people singing. It was around Christmas time, and there was a group of white people singing *O Come All Ye Faithful* underneath a tree outside the church. At that moment,' he says, 'I felt an incredible sense of grace. Just by hearing these people sing—people divided from my people by history – hearing them sing under a tree on my land, connected me with them through God. I never even had to say anything to them,' Stan says, 'to find that moment of grace.'

FURTHER READING

Stan Grant, *The Queen is Dead: The Time Has Come for a Reckoning*, HarperCollins, 2023

Stan Grant, 'This is the way healing begins: Recovering the language of lament in a disenchanted age', *ABC Religion and Ethics*, 21 August 2023 (online)

Stan Grant, *With the Falling of the Dusk: a Chronicle of the World in Crisis*, HarperCollins, 2021

Stan Grant, *Talking to My Country*, HarperCollins, 2017

Rufus Black

Rufus Black is Vice-Chancellor of the University of Tasmania. He holds degrees in law, politics, economics, ethics and theology from the University of Melbourne and Oxford University, where he studied as a Rhodes Scholar. After a career in consulting, he returned to academia at the University of Melbourne where he was Master of Ormond College. During this time, he co-led the creation of a Master of Entrepreneurship and taught as an Enterprise Professor in the Department of Management and Marketing. He was also a Principal Fellow in the University of Melbourne's Department of Philosophy and taught as lead faculty for the Centre for Ethical Leadership. He has made a broad range of contributions to the community, including having been President of Museums Victoria, Deputy Chancellor of Victoria University, a non-executive director of the Walter and Eliza Hall Institute of Medical Research and of Innovation Science Australia, and the founding Chair of the Board of Teach for Australia. Rufus's research and writing have been published widely, including by Oxford University Press and Routledge and he has authored a number of major public reports for the Australian Government.

RUFUS BLACK'S CAREER began, in a sense, with a question. It was his first year at university, and a Professor of Economics was explaining utilitarianism: a moral outlook which says that the right thing to do in any given situation is to choose the option that will maximise utility. An implication of this way of thinking is that what counts as 'utility' can be measured and calculated and compared.

The young Rufus Black disagreed.

'I thought it was intellectually bankrupt,' he says today. 'It was immediately apparent to me that the idea that you could reduce things to utility, and create some kind of utilitarian ranking of things, could not be right.' Rufus's father was a lawyer who had worked on several important environmental cases, and his mother was an artist. The memory of many childhood holidays in the natural world helped him to formulate a question for his professor: 'I asked how you could rank, for example, a piece of unseen Lemonthyme forest against a piece of unseen Daintree rainforest? How could you conceivably figure out any way in which one is preferable, or better than the other, or has greater utility?'

The professor admitted this was a very good question. In fact, he needed to go away and think about it. He came back the next week. 'I've thought about your question,' he said, 'and I just can't answer it. It's simply a premise of economics – if you want to study economics, you need to accept this premise.'

This wasn't a very satisfying answer, but it planted a seed. Several years later, Rufus Black completed a DPhil in moral theology as a Rhodes Scholar at the University of Oxford. He says today: 'The question of finding a non-utilitarian solution to economic and social questions was central to my doctoral studies. My whole university journey had been a conversation between the understandings of value that were coming out of my religious explorations, meeting, rather unhappily, the understandings of value I was finding in the university curricula.'

Today, Rufus Black is Vice-Chancellor of the University of Tasmania, but the path there has been long and varied: before heading to Tasmania, he was Master of Ormond College at the University of Melbourne as well as an Enterprise Professor in the

Department of Management and Marketing and a Principal Fellow in the Department of Philosophy. For nine years before that he was a partner at McKinsey and Company and a Director of the law firm Corrs Chambers Westgarth. He has conducted several reviews for Federal and State Governments, including the Prime Minister's Independent Review of the Australian Intelligence Community. This is not the usual path someone would take after studying theology at Oxford, but Rufus insists that theology plays a role in everything he does. 'I feel very grateful for the quality of theological education I got,' he says. 'There would barely be a day of my professional life when it's not informing what I do.' The question he asked in first-year economics, and his concern not to reduce the world to measurement and utility, is a theme that has played out throughout his career. Rufus Black's working life since university is, he tells us, a story of 'two different constructs of reality engaging creatively with one another.'

One of these constructs was imbued early. Christian theologians sometimes talk about the 'two books' in which God is revealed: the Bible, and creation itself. Throughout his childhood, Rufus was steeped in both books. 'I can't remember a time,' he says, 'when I didn't have some sense that there was a larger Other around which you had to make sense of the world. Somewhere along the line a name – God – got put to that.' And visits to the natural world played a role? 'Yes, nature has always been part of it. For me, it's particularly connected to the sea. In my spirituality, the ocean as a metaphor for God has been an important theme.'

The other book – Scripture – also featured, and in a particularly intense way. 'As a child, I read a story in which the main character was advised by his parents to make sure he reads the Bible every day. I thought, that's good advice. So I started on page one of Genesis and just kept reading. Right through my pre-teenage and teenage years, I just kept patiently reading the thing from front to back – I think about three times overall.' That's not something most Christians have done: how did it shape Rufus's spirituality? 'The Bible gave me, in all of its glorious diversity, an extraordinary resource to call on. The ability to see the world through the narratives and poems, the imagery, the arc of the history of Israel. These are lenses through which to view the world, and I find them to be endlessly generative.' Familiarity with the Jewish and Christian scriptures also helps make sense of the cultural world in which we live, Rufus says. 'For years I've dealt with students who can't see their own history. There's a huge amount of their own cultural heritage which is unknown to them. That's a real tragedy, I think. Whether you're religious or not, to have great chunks of the last 2000 years of history rendered almost opaque or incomprehensible is a pretty bad thing.'

Not everyone who has studied theology can explain how it informs their life and work, but Rufus Black is a very systematic thinker. He names four ways in which theology has made a difference over an eclectic career.

First, he says, it provided him with an alternative to the kind of utilitarian thinking espoused by his first-year economics professor. 'Studying theology helped me to develop a truly robust, non-utilitarian account of ethics and human society.' What's the alternative to utilitarianism? 'I'm a natural law theorist in the tradition of people like John Finnis and Germaine Grisez, even if I disagree with them about some of the practical applications of natural law theory, particularly around gender and sexuality.'

Natural law theory involves thinking about ethics as emerging from the kinds of creatures human beings are: rather than trying to identify a measure of value and then maximising it, the natural law theorist thinks about what human beings need to live healthy and flourishing lives, and to live these *together*, in communities. 'Natural law theory has given me a comprehensive, non-utilitarian way of understanding how decisions can and should be made,' says Rufus. 'It helps to make sense of things economics can't.'

The second thing theology has given Rufus Black is a strong sense of the importance of our relationships with one another. 'The doctrine of the Trinity,' he says, 'means that the fundamental nature of reality is relationality.' Christian teaching about the Trinity says that God, while not being made up of parts, is nonetheless a relationship between three distinct persons: the Father, the Son and the Holy Spirit. It's a very difficult teaching to understand, but according to Rufus it means that *relationship* is somehow at the heart of things – not an optional extra. 'Relationality is what you've got to constantly seek, which means you can't reduce things to the transactional.' For Rufus, former British Prime Minister Margaret Thatcher's famous declaration that 'there is no such thing as society' is 'the logical end of the transactional world'. 'A theme of everything I've done,' he says, 'is to try to find ways to make relationality work.' How? 'One part of the answer is finding common purpose in pursuit of the good. A transaction is a mutual exchange, but a collaboration is about finding our common ground before the worthwhile thing that we're doing together. This doesn't mean the world isn't full of transactions. But it's not reduced to that. For me, that's why the Trinity is really important.'

The third important theological theme in Rufus's life comes from the doctrine of the Incarnation: the idea that God became human in Jesus. 'The doctrine of the Incarnation is really about the capacity for wholeness in a world full of brokenness. The most important image for me is the wounds on the resurrected Christ. Jesus is made whole, but not by taking the wounds away. Wholeness isn't a denial of the messiness of human life – its brutality at times, its awfulness. The incarnation is the hope that despite all of that we can still engage in making things whole.' How does this insight affect the way Rufus goes about things? 'It helps me to be understanding of the messiness of human life. In whatever I'm doing – whether it's working in an organisation or designing public policy – I need to accommodate that messiness. I can't be utopian.'

The fourth thing theology has given Rufus is a profound commitment to coherence. Almost by definition, theology is about how things hold together in God. 'Theology is like geography,' says Rufus. 'It's fundamentally premised on the belief in a coherent whole. We may never understand the whole – in fact we can't, and there's a humility in that. But theology allows a constant attempt to render the world coherent, and I've never stopped trying to do that. Every single day I'm asking: how do I make sense of this? You can't ask that question if you don't start from the premise that sense is possible.'

Rufus adds: 'This is not just an intellectual exercise for me. In my personal life, I've encountered great evil; I've seen how bad the world can be and the terrible toll it can take on people. That presence of evil is ultimately the strongest foundation for atheism, I think. I've had to find meaning in some very dark places, and theology has helped me to do that.'

It's fascinating to hear how Rufus sees his task as one of bringing two constructs of reality together – applying his theological world view to questions in business, academia, government and public life. But do we need theology to do this? Can't we just come up with an ethical alternative to utilitarianism that doesn't involve theological premises? 'Natural law can be done without needing to reference God,' Rufus agrees. 'But to understand the full depth of what you're engaging with requires a theological lens. My doctoral thesis deals directly with the question: does God make a difference? I think if you believe in God, your obligations change. Let's take the simplest example. If you believe you're forgiven in an unconditional way for the various wrongs you've done, then your duties to other people are different. If you accept God's generosity, you can't go around treating people the way you would if you didn't have that as your reality. If you are not similarly generous, then you're fundamentally ethically inconsistent. The reality of God is a reality that changes how you live in the world, fundamentally.'

As an ordained Uniting Church minister, Rufus Black has employed his theological training in ministry. But most of his work has been outside of the church. 'The theology I studied at Oxford,' he says, 'I have to transact, mostly, in an entirely secular universe. I have to find non-Christian language to do this. I've often described my job as being a translator: how do we translate these deep theological understandings into secular conversations?'

There are a number of examples of his attempts to do this. For nine years, he worked at McKinsey and Company, a large multinational corporate consulting firm. Here, he says, 'my theological studies gave me a way to understand corporate decision-making as infinitely more sophisticated than just profit-maximising choices.' In a world in which companies are increasingly aware of their responsibilities to the environment and to the communities in which they operate, the ability to understand human beings as more than customers, more than simple rational economic actors, was valuable. 'I think that being able to tease out the non-economic drivers of people's decisions – and natural law theory is all about the values being pursued and the principles to pursue them – made me really effective,' Rufus says. 'It was a toolkit others didn't have: I could identify what values were at stake. When you're in the world of economic management, having a richer anthropology sets you up really well.'

An example: 'I was working with a telecommunications company, looking at how certain technologies were used in rural Australia and what their future might be. I was able to say, look, let's not start from whether this makes you money or not. Let's start by asking: what are the humanly important things that this technology makes possible? It reduces isolation, it creates community. In the end, that's what really matters – and we were able to build the strategy from that starting point.'

A theological perspective has also helped Rufus in his work for government, in particular for the Department of Defence. 'The department was revising its approach to ethics,' he says, 'and it was going in what I saw as an intellectually incoherent, quasi-utilitarian direction. I was able to introduce a natural law account of ethics, which really changed the conversation. The department's new approach reflected this understanding in a way that it didn't before.' It can't be easy to change a large organisation's ethical framework. 'No, it was an arm wrestle,' Rufus admits. 'But we had a comprehensive win!'

Rufus Black now lives in Tasmania, where he is Vice-Chancellor of that state's university. It's another entirely secular environment but his theological training, he says, 'has been helpful in sorting out what the mission of the university is.' 'Mission', of course, is originally a theological concept – and determining mission is about asking the right questions: 'Do we want to continue on a globalised model of higher education? Or do we want to be a place-based university? Are we premised on a growth model or a quest for a sustainable size? How do we ensure that access, excellence and originality are not in tension? These are all existential questions for a university,' says Rufus, 'and they contain a whole bunch of theological implications. The language, the constructs I use are all grounded in my theological construction of the world.'

Does theology help you do things in a different way, or does it give you different things to do? It's a bit of both, says Rufus. Sometimes, Christianity must 'disrupt' the world. 'There are occasions when Christianity gives you the ability to act out of love and reconciliation in ways which have nothing to do with the secular system.' What does this look like in a university setting? 'For me the most powerful example was when we apologised to Aboriginal people for the things we had done to them over the length of our history.'

The Palawa people of lutruwita (Tasmania) suffered greatly from the European invasion of the land we now call Australia. They experienced massacres, forced resettlement, even the denial of their existence on the island. On 4 December 2019, Rufus Black stood with his Chancellor and other staff and admitted that the University he ran had been built on the proceeds of war and dispossession. He noted that Aboriginal artefacts and even the bodies of Aboriginal people had not been treated with respect. 'For too long,' he said, 'the histories we taught hid the true story of war and genocidal behaviour. For too long, the wisdom of Aboriginal people was not thought worthy of our academy.' He then apologised in English and in *palawa kani*, a language that had almost been lost before being reconstructed from old records and recordings.

'My understanding of what we were doing on that day,' Rufus tells us, 'was born out of a reconciliation narrative. It's not about justice – not the secular model of justice – because the wrongs are so deep in the past. The only path forward is a kind of radical breaking into secular politics of a reconciliation that is only possible because of the extraordinary generosity that might be there. If you take the risk of seeking forgiveness, the answer might be "No, we don't accept your apology." But the Christian experience of reconciliation means you can do a radically apolitical act, which is probably the only way you can heal human relationships. So we apologised, and it was a really profound thing to do. And it didn't come out of the normal politics of a secular university.'

As someone who has been formed by the study of theology, in nature and in scripture and in formal education, and as someone who has brought what he has learned into many different roles, what does Rufus think is the future of theological education in Australia? 'Theology needs to start with Aboriginal understandings of the relationship between all things,' he says. 'Aboriginal people understand reality in a deeply relational way.' This resonates with our earlier discussion about the doctrine of the Trinity. 'From the late middle ages Western thought has been crippled by the divide between the object and the subject,' Rufus says. 'This has been useful for science and some other purposes, but it can disconnect us from nature, and in many cases it has done so.'

How can engaging with Aboriginal people and spirituality help? 'One of the genuine pleasures of my life,' says Rufus, 'has been to engage with Aboriginal people. It's a spiritual space where I feel very much at home. A great weaknesses of Christian theology is that it often doesn't have a good understanding of the gift of creation. We don't tend to respond to nature as sheer giftedness. We need to reconceptualise how we can operate sustainably on the planet. The relationship between Aboriginal people and country, as I have experienced it, is a connectivity between all things: a non-separation between country and person. It's a participation in a spiritual universe whose realities are manifest in country, if you have eyes to see.'

Has the church managed to do this at all? 'I think one of the great failings of Australian Christianity – and I'm afraid there are many – has been not to engage, not to be reformed by encounters with Aboriginal and Torres Strait Islander peoples and with the ecology of our entire continent. We should be remade by our continent theologically. This would reconnect us to some pre-modern thinking that would ultimately be theologically renewing. We would understand our own narratives in new and different ways. We have to be cured of modernity, because modernity is killing us and killing the planet. I see the Australian church as, absurdly, dying in a place which is full of resources for its renewal. Insofar as Aboriginal people are generous enough to let us listen, we could well do with a decade of listening.'

Despite his serious criticisms of the church in Australia, Rufus Black remains a participant in church life. 'For all my frustration with the churches, I've never given up, because once you have a God who's engaged with the community, rather than concerned only to save individuals, this actually creates a collective mission and we have to engage with that.'

FURTHER READING

Rufus Black, *Christian Moral Realism: Natural Law, Narrative, Virtue, and the Gospel* (Oxford Theology and Religion Monographs), Clarendon Press, 2001

Rufus Black et. al., *Ethics at War: How Should Military Personnel Make Ethical Decisions?*, Routledge, 2023

Deborah Barker

Deborah Barker is Principal of St Kevin's College in Melbourne. Previously, she has been Principal at Santa Maria College, Northcote, Deputy Principal at Our Lady of Sion College, Box Hill, and Director of Faith and Mission at Mount Lilydale Mercy College, Lilydale. Deborah has a Bachelor of Education, a Bachelor of Theology from the Melbourne College of Divinity, a Masters in Educational Leadership from the University of Melbourne, and she finished studies at Harvard University in 2017.

Deborah Barker always wanted to be a teacher. 'For me,' she says, 'as a young child, play meant a blackboard and dolls.' In January 2021, she was appointed principal of St Kevin's College in Toorak. Deborah brought to the role not only a wealth of experience, and extensive training in education and leadership, but also a Bachelor of Theology. How did this come about?

'Early in my career, I took on a Year Ten religious education class,' she tells us. 'These were 15-year-olds, and the questions they were asking me were extraordinary.' Such as? 'They weren't asking about the seven sacraments: these were big questions about the meaning of life and life's purpose. Also questions from their own experiences. For example: My Auntie just got cancer. How can you say that God is loving? These were great, great questions.'

But there was a problem: 'I didn't know the answers. How could I deal with these questions as a new teacher only three or four years out? It forced me to think – well, what do I believe? What's my understanding of my own Catholic belief and my experience? So I decided to study some theology.' Did you find the answers you were looking for? 'Of course not! But what theology gave me was a framework: a really rich framework in which to think, teach and act.'

Young people also need a framework: they are subject to increasing stresses, pressures, claims and counter-claims, expectations and responsibilities. When we spoke to Deborah Barker, we were interested to learn how theological education informed her efforts to lead the community at St Kevin's, a 105-year-old Catholic boys' school. One theological theme cropped up early and resurfaced throughout our conversation: hope.

'People say to me: Deborah, you're always using the word "hope",' she tells us. 'I insist I also talk about solidarity and community and love and forgiveness! They say, yes – but you keep coming back to hope.' It's an especially important virtue to impart to a generation who spent a chunk of their childhoods in COVID lockdown. Compounding any lingering sense of anxiety from this period is the knowledge that they are entering a world of crisis, conflict and climate change – and a world that is more interconnected than ever before. 'We live in a global village,' says Deborah, 'where young people are exposed to so much.' As we speak, the world is bombarded with images and reports from the war in Ukraine, surely the most extensively broadcast war in history.

'I think young people are wondering, what are these adults doing?' Deborah goes on. 'They have questions around authority – in fact, they have a distrust in authority.' She agrees this may be justified given the track record of authorities over the past few years. 'Young people are asking: what have the adults of previous generations done about climate change? Do we have to do everything? At 15 or 16, they are being asked to make judgments on big adult human decisions and human meaning and purpose.'

Theology, says Deborah, is 'a framework we can give students to be critical, to sift through what they are hearing.' It's not about handing out answers, but rather helping students to ask good questions – and it must be made relevant to the situation students find themselves in. 'We need to help students connect theology with the world as it is,' Deborah says. This is not simply done by repeating the official line on issues such as climate change; but we can, says Deborah, offer a range of perspectives, including religious perspectives: 'Here's what some significant people in the world are saying. Here's what Pope Francis is saying.' Like so many people around the world, religious and otherwise, students can find great value in the current Pope's reflections on the climate crisis.

'Theology can help us open up a bigger conversation,' Deborah continues, 'but young people need to experience religious faith at their own level. We should look at the language and images we use for a start.' Another caveat: 'Young people have to come to the table as equals. They should have respect for adults, because adults do have life experience and acquired knowledge. But the pedagogy of teaching is different to what it was 30 years ago when I started. It's about inquiry. It's about working together. It's about collaboration and problem solving. It's not about being told, and done to. This change can be hard for a hierarchical church, yet the synodal way of Pope Francis offers real possibilities here.'

Deborah is the first woman ever to hold the position of principal at St Kevin's College – but she doesn't tend to think in those terms. 'I come as a person who is female. I often look at things through a feminist lens, but I'm first and foremost an educator. The boys just accept me as Mrs Barker, who's now their principal. For me, gender is not the issue. I'm an experienced principal who was appointed because of the skill set, leadership and experience I bring. It's true that female leaders still have to work really, really hard – much harder than their male counterparts to reach an equivalent position. But I look forward to the day when people see me, and all people, as people.'

Does theology help or hinder the feminist cause? 'I think we need to ask how we honour the feminine, the female,' Deborah says. 'What metaphors, what symbols do we use? What imagery are we using for God, for example? In studying Scripture, we find some wonderful female characters such as Ruth, Naomi and Sarah, and yet they are often unknown. There's plenty in there and we just need to unearth it: the notion of wisdom, for example, the femininity of God. That's where theology is helpful. One of the reasons I love education is that we can contribute to allowing young people to unearth what is already there, and help them see things in new ways, perhaps even counter-cultural ways.'

Deborah has also identified an often under-appreciated resource in the Catholic school system. Many schools, including St Kevin's, were founded by religious orders, and every religious order operates out of what is called a 'charism'. This is an old-fashioned term but it comes from a Greek word meaning 'gift' and describes the particular spiritual focus of the order. 'I've always wanted to work in schools with a charism,' says Deborah. 'Obviously any Catholic school is based first and foremost on the person, mission, life, death and resurrection of Jesus Christ. It's Jesus first, but to be able to navigate and narrate through the lens of a particular charism is incredibly enriching.'

One example of a charism is that of the Sisters of Our Lady of Sion, who founded Our Lady of Sion College, where Deborah Barker has worked. Originally focused on serving and being in dialogue with Jewish people, the charism broadened to be about interfaith dialogue, peace and justice in general. Deborah found this to be particularly influential: 'To be in a community where you learn, not only about your own Christian tradition, but also about Judaism and Islam and so on – that openness to other faiths really opens up a sense of what it means to live in our current world.'

Immediately before coming to St Kevin's, Deborah experienced another charism at work. Santa Maria College, where she was principal, was founded by the Sisters of the Good Samaritan, whose charism is based on the teachings of St Benedict of Nursia. Benedict is one of the Christian world's greatest teachers on monastic life – but what does a sixth-century monk have to offer to a modern Australian girls' school? 'Benedict offers timeless writings on how to work with people and how to see God,' says Deborah. 'When I was at Santa Maria College, we asked, what does it mean to live in a Benedictine community?'

There are Benedictine communities all around the world: women and men living lives of prayer, work, contemplation and community. 'Benedict is about being in the present, and being a presence,' says Deborah. 'It's about being quiet at times but also enjoying community, and working with each other in community. At Santa Maria College, we introduced meditation. Just after morning tea the whole school would be called to silence for a couple of minutes. It didn't matter where you were, you would hear the bell and stop.' And what did this do for the school? 'You would have a sense of being present to the other, present to God. For the students, it was great, and the teachers loved it because the students would come to their next class more focused, calmed down.'

As a relatively new principal to St Kevin's, Deborah is still exploring the charism of St Kevin's College. The school was founded in 1918 by the Christian Brothers, whose charism comes from their founder, Blessed Edmund Rice. 'Edmund Rice was about caring for those on the margins,' says Deborah. 'If we are serious about being in the Edmund Rice tradition, that's what we're called to do.' She quotes the Australian saint Mary Mackillop: 'Never see a need without doing something about it.'

At a time when the members of many religious orders are aging and unable to continue, it's encouraging to see how their founding energies, their spiritual resources, can be captured, harnessed and handed on in the school communities they founded. Each charism, says Deborah, 'provides a unique opportunity for the community of faith to ask, how do we look at the Jesus story through this lens?' The concept of charism does not belong in the past. The founders of religious orders were inspired by their vision of God and the world to serve a particular need. A question for any religiously-based educational organisation today is how to create an environment in which young people can reflect and make a difference.

Speaking to Deborah, it's clear that schools are at the forefront of the big social (and therefore theological) questions facing Australia today. Schools are actually doing what Pope Francis has encouraged the Catholic Church to do: meet people where they are, in the messiness and joys of their lives. For example, churches still wrestle with their response to people who do not fit in with traditional views about gender and sexuality. Deborah tells us: 'This is a big current issue for schools. And schools are actually navigating it. For a variety of reasons, which I understand, the church hierarchies are not being proactive in this space – but schools are.' What does that look like on the ground? 'Particularly in Catholic schools, people are enrolled and employed and included because of who they are as people. This means there always has to be a respectful understanding of people's stories. People must not feel rejected in any way, shape or form. That's the challenge. How can we say as a community that we are inclusive, we are loving, we are compassionate and empathetic – and yet we reject people?' Deborah is blunt about this. 'We can't.'

Deborah Barker has had some difficult but ultimately life-giving conversations with families wrestling with this issue. 'It's a sacred time when you're sitting around a table with a family talking about this – it's an encounter, a God moment.' But it's still not an easy issue for a Catholic school. 'We work with families and students so they can continue to be educated within our tradition, and continue to feel that they are loved. How do you do this when you've got people in the community saying other things? That's when you need some clear defining principles. We continue to work in partnership with the church on this.' Deborah acknowledges the tensions involved in a large, global church with many different views and life experiences when it comes to matters of sexual orientation. 'We've got to journey together on this one. We need to love these young people. And we also need to think about how to bring along people who are finding this really difficult to accept.'

There are many reasons to study theology, and Deborah Barker found a particularly good one in her need to engage with young people's questions about life, the world and ultimate sources of meaning. 'It was the students' questions that created the drive in me to go and find the answers, so that I could provide them with a framework for thinking and somehow journey with them.' Deborah is now a strong supporter of teachers being encouraged and supported to pursue theological studies. 'Theology allowed me to be open, to ask questions; to not be restricted, but rather widened and broadened. It opened up new horizons. One of the critical contributions Catholic Education can make is the provision of ongoing theological study for teachers.' It also affected her own faith. 'Life brings so many struggles and joys and possibilities. Theology provided me with knowledge that assisted my own wonderings and reflection and prayer life. It allowed me to challenge some of the things that I was hearing. It helped me feel more liberated.' Theological institutions can offer this to students, too. Not only a framework for thinking and acting, but also the opportunity to think big, to think in a liberated way, to take risks.

When asked for any final thoughts, Deborah comes back once again to hope. 'There are always glimpses of hope. Look for it, take the opportunities to see it, and be grateful for things that are good. Make sure you see goodness in the world, because there is great goodness in the world, and great goodness in our communities. Hold on to it. We're all made in the likeness and image of God. In my belief system, there are God moments, there are glimpses of hope. And in Jesus we meet hope.'

Kevin Rudd

Born and raised in country Queensland, Kevin Rudd became Australia's 26th Prime Minister in 2007 after leading the Australian Labor Party into government after more than eleven years in opposition. He served as Prime Minister from 2007 to 2010, and again in 2013. He was also Australia's Foreign Minister between 2010 and 2012. A global authority on China, the Australian Government announced in December 2022 that he would be appointed Australia's Ambassador to the United States in Washington DC.

KEVIN RUDD DIDN'T GO to university when he finished high school; at least not straight away. Why not? 'I didn't know what I believed in.'

The Hon. Dr Kevin Rudd AC, 26th Prime Minister of Australia, now Australian Ambassador to the United States, began his post-school life wandering around the country, picking up odd jobs where he could, thinking about the world and his place in it. 'It wasn't that I didn't know what I wanted to do,' he says today. 'In fact I had a clear idea about what I wanted to do: I wanted to become a lawyer, and I thought I'd like to study China.' But something else had to come first.

Kevin Rudd's mother was devoutly Catholic: her religion was, as he describes it, 'traditional Irish Catholic provincial Queensland – post the Split.' Many older Australians will immediately recognise this description; younger ones might need a breakdown. The Labor 'Split' occurred during the Cold War in the 1950s when many Catholics, who were traditionally Labor voters and often party members as well, quit the party in response to its perceived accommodating attitude to communism. They formed the Democratic Labor Party and kept the ALP out of power for the next couple of decades. It was a traumatic time in Labor politics, and religion was soaked right through.

The traditional side of Margaret Rudd's Catholic faith manifested itself in regular Mass attendance and family rosary once or twice a week. 'As the youngest child, I got to lie on the bed for the rosary,' says Kevin, 'because I was too little to kneel beside it. This caused considerable angst on the part of my siblings.' 'Provincial Queensland' in many cases meant poor, or at least working class; which is why, in Kevin's words, his decision not to go to university 'freaked my mother out.' He had been dux of his year at school. 'Put yourself in the mind of a working-class Catholic woman from the Queensland countryside,' he says, 'whose kid is qualified to go to university – and decides not to.'

When his wanderings led him to Sydney, Rudd started visiting churches each Sunday. 'I really hadn't spent any time in a Protestant church before,' he says. 'I remember going to the Central Methodist Mission; to Pitt St Congregational Church; to Scots Presbyterian Church and to local Churches of Christ not far from where I lived. I would dip in and out, often stay for a few weeks and then move on elsewhere.'

What was he looking for, and what did he find? Rudd paraphrases St Augustine's famous address to God, which in the original reads: 'You have formed us for yourself, and our hearts are restless till they find rest in you.' Rudd's version: 'I know that I am incomplete and I can only be complete in you.' He tells us that his move into Christian faith was 'not the classic thing of "I woke up one morning and discovered what a sinful person I was."'

Rather, 'it was a sense of incompleteness, followed by a sense of completeness.'

Though not formally trained in theology, Kevin Rudd is steeped in it. Australians got a taste of this when, while in Opposition in 2006, he wrote a long essay for *The Monthly* magazine about the twentieth-century German theologian Dietrich Bonhoeffer. (He remembers the look of 'blank incomprehension' on political journalist Kerry O'Brien's face when he named Bonhoeffer as his most admired leader in an early TV interview.) Bonhoeffer lived in Germany during the rise of the Nazis, and was eventually put to death in a concentration camp for his involvement in a plot against Hitler. As Rudd writes in his essay, Bonhoeffer pushed back against the Lutheran 'Two Kingdoms' doctrine, according to which the Kingdom of God need not, and should not, have much to do with the kingdom of this world. This doctrine, according to Bonhoeffer, permitted a quietist response by many church leaders to the rise of the Nazi regime. The alternative to the 'Two Kingdoms' approach is for the church and Christians to engage with politics – something Kevin Rudd supports and has exemplified throughout his career.

'Christians in politics is a vexed business,' he admits, 'because politics in the secular state – and I defend the secular state – is always about the business of compromise between conflicting interests. Christians in the secular state have always got to be mindful of the moral voice, to bring people back to fundamental questions of informed conscience on the way through. But you can't fully answer those questions unless you're prepared to fully throw yourself into the fray as well.'

Kevin threw himself into the fray, but that came later. He did, of course, eventually go to university, graduating from the Australian National University with a major in Chinese language and history. As a young diplomat, Kevin lived in China, where despite speaking Mandarin, 'we chose not to go to a Chinese church, because as a student of Chinese human rights I did not want to compromise the safety of the Chinese adherents.' His honours thesis was on the imprisoned democracy activist Wei Jingsheng. 'That's why we were careful to remain members of the International Christian Fellowship.' His local church was an 'all hands on deck' affair: without priests or ministers, the congregation basically ran the church. This included preaching: 'I spoke there on a number of occasions, as did others.'

How does Rudd think about the task of preaching, and how does it compare with the kind of public speaking that is more familiar to him today – political speechmaking? To answer this question he turns to the eighteenth-century founders of the Methodist movement, John and Charles Wesley. 'I've always been taken by Wesleyan sermonology,' Kevin says, 'and Wesleyan hymnology for that matter – and there's a relationship between them.' John Wesley's sermons, he explains, operate by 'the discipline of three points, and three points in sequence.' Charles Wesley's hymns work in a similar way. 'If you look carefully at [the hymn] "And Can it Be", for example,' says Rudd, 'it's not a series of random observations put to a pleasant tune; it's the exposition of a systematic message.'

'The reason John and Charles Wesley did it so well together,' he continues, 'is that they understood the importance of simplifying the message, making the message logical, and making it memorable. What is the parallel between that and political speechmaking?' He repeats: 'Simplicity of the message; providing a narrative which takes you across the terrain; and – to lift directly from the Wesleys – giving the people a tune to hum.'

As an example he mentions the Apology to the Stolen Generations, which he delivered in the Australian Parliament on 13 February 2008. It was one of his earliest acts as Prime

Minister – a long overdue response to a 1997 inquiry which described the terrible impact on First Nations children, families and communities of the forced removal of children from their families. Rudd wrote the apology in longhand after spending an afternoon with an elderly survivor of the Stolen Generations, Lorna 'Nanna Nungala' Feio. The Wesleyan influence can be seen throughout. 'If you look at the construction of the Apology,' Kevin says, 'it's not a series of random observations. It seeks to build a case, it concludes the case, apologises, and then proceeds from the "theology" of apology to the praxis of reconciliation through Closing the Gap.'

Indeed, the Apology has a liturgical flavour about it, with its repetition of words and phrases and its narrative of confession, repentance and hope. Kevin Rudd believes 'there is a connection between the spiritual and the political at the level of language' and points to the King James version of the Bible, whose translators 'understood full well the rhythms of Shakespearean English, and understood that to craft a sentence and to craft a paragraph was as much about weighting and rhythm as it was about the actual content of the language within.'

Kevin Rudd still thinks about Australia's relationship with its First Peoples in theological terms. 'I think the first response must always be to listen, respect, and to learn from their underlying spirituality, particularly their spirituality of place, the epigenetics of Indigenous spirituality. The feeling and experience of place and sacredness which comes from millennia – tens of millennia – of the pre-Christian world is something for us all as Christians to reflect upon with a great deal of humility.'

For many years, First Nations people have been calling for a treaty in Australia. 'I think what theology would say to us,' says Rudd, 'is that human compassion is not a reflection of human weakness, it's a reflection of human strength. Therefore choosing to form a treaty with each other is an expression of human strength, not human weakness. Because a treaty is able to embrace the terms of our engagement, rather than brushing under the uncomfortable rug of human history the violent and brutal details of the European arrival and the attempted extermination of large slabs of Indigenous Australia.'

Kevin remembers being in Cape Town a few years ago with the now late Archbishop Desmond Tutu, who reminded him of the importance of 'staring truth squarely in the face, and truth telling about all of that, hanging all of it out on the line, the dirty stuff as well, calling it for what it is, and agreeing on our terms of engagement for the future. That's why a process of treaty making is important, and important theologically as well. It's a form of covenantal relationship.'

It's rare to hear a former Prime Minister speak in these terms. Some might find it uncomfortable, or even inappropriate. Others might think that explicit Christian commitment traditionally belongs on the conservative side of Australian politics, not the Labor side. But from his early days as Leader of the Opposition, Kevin Rudd was determined to emphasise that God is not a 'wholly-owned subsidiary of the Liberal Party.' In a more recent article he wrote that 'My simple, garden-variety theology is this: the God of the New Testament gives preference to the poor, the outcast and the oppressed and, to the greatest extent possible, I should do the same, while also being a good custodian of the planet.'

What might this look like in political terms? Rudd has thought deeply (and written many times) about the relationship between church and state. He notes the ways in which contemporary liberal democratic political norms and institutions have been shaped by Christian belief. 'The ethical precepts of Christianity had a profound effect on Western politics and western statecraft by delegitimising the use of large scale violence. It did not eliminate violence, but if you were to ask the pre-Christian world what their view was of violence – whether it was the violence of the arena in late Republican/early Imperial Rome, or other forms of state-authorised, state-accepted or state-embraced violence – there was nothing inherently wrong with it. There were laws against murder, but violence against slaves or against people beyond the tribe was just normal.'

Later, he says, 'Christianity gave rise to a view that compassion should not simply be an individual philanthropic gesture but should take the form and shape of creating institutions for looking after the poor and the sick and the orphaned, and so gave rise to the first dispensaries, for example, the first schools, and, as a result, suddenly you see a different impact of the church on the state. I think a third impact comes from the tradition of the Christian socialists of the nineteenth century.' He names some of the politicians influenced by this movement, including the Australian Prime Minister Andrew Fisher (in office 1914-15), and one of the founders of the British Labour Party, Keir Hardie. Rudd has also called himself an 'old-fashioned Christian socialist'. This tradition insists that 'beyond individual philanthropic acts, beyond creating philanthropic institutions, the state itself should give effect to social justice by creating public hospitals for the poor, public schools for the poor, aged pensions for the poor, and so on.'

If the modern state has been so profoundly shaped by Christianity, what is the role of the churches today? Given his many years in public office, Kevin Rudd's answer is a little surprising. 'I think the job of the contemporary church, and contemporary Christianity,' he says, 'is to make the state feel as ethically uncomfortable with itself as possible.' How? 'The job of the church, in the tradition of Bonhoeffer, is constantly to say: what about the refugee? And what about the drug addict? And what about the poor? And what about the sick? The job is constantly to hang a moral lantern on the problem, and to make the state always feel uncomfortable about the secular compromises which it is required to make in order to sustain the apparatus of the state, and the orderly governance of the state.' He insists that the church should 'never be subsumed by the state. Never captured by the state. Never co-opted by the state.'

But there is a caveat. Christianity may have had a positive impact on the state historically, but there is also a much darker legacy. 'It's pretty hard to walk around the world these days,' says Kevin, 'and not conclude the quantum damage the church has done to itself through the abuse of minors. It's not exclusively a Catholic phenomenon, although the Catholic Church has a huge share of it.'

How can the churches regain enough credibility to speak once again into the public conversation? 'The global reflection that the Catholic Church, and the combined Christian churches, need to have on this monumental act of ethical hypocrisy, has to have the same collective truth-telling conclusion we've already spoken about in terms of the relationship between Indigenous Australians and white Australians, or first nations and settler communities around the world.' This sounds like a massive task but for Kevin Rudd it is essential. 'The moral clarity of the voice of the church speaking across the ages is pulled apart by this [legacy of abuse]. A new beginning is needed on these questions so that the voice can be heard again.' He adds: 'The voices of women are important to reconstitute the ethical voice of the church, because most of the abuses come from men.'

Recently in Canberra, Kevin Rudd attended the unveiling of his official prime ministerial portrait by the artist Ralph Heimans. In it he is pictured in his library, a book open in front of him, with a chess board mid-way through a game, his cat knocking over one of the pieces. The chess board is not an accident. Since studying

China as an undergraduate, Kevin Rudd has observed and analysed the shifting geopolitical realities affecting Australia and the world. Amid the celebratory atmosphere of his portrait unveiling, he took the opportunity to warn that 'we are in a region where the risk of crisis, conflict and war is real – not a theory, it's a real threat.' He has been warning of this for some time. In 2022, Rudd published *The Avoidable War: The Dangers of a Catastrophic Conflict between the US and Xi Jinping's China*. It is a thorough, learned analysis of the positions and perceptions of both sides, and outlines a practical path to avoiding what could potentially be the worst military conflict in the history of the world. The book is not a theological book; but it is itself an act of peacemaking, something with deep theological resonance.

We asked Kevin Rudd how Christians and church communities can help to make peace today. 'I think the role of the church in reflecting on war and peace,' he tells us, 'is constantly to bring into sharp focus the appalling human cost of war – in graphic ways – for the international secular community to confront before triggers are pulled.' But, he says, 'when violence is committed against another state, the church should not be morally squeamish about the right to national self-defence as articulated in the UN Charter.' So calling for peace is not enough? The church should not, Kevin says, 'just be a bunch of international pacifists, because if you're a bunch of international pacifists, guess what? Totalitarians regard you as a walkover. If and when the balloon goes up, and, for example, effective deterrence fails, then [Christians should] not be morally squeamish about defending against wars of aggression. I think there's a fairly clear theology about that.'

Rudd has little time for those who criticise politics from the outside without engaging closely with political realities. The church's challenge today, he says, is 'to harness longstanding and relatively clear-cut ethical positions on the narrow legitimisations of the use of violence; to advance the cause of the intrinsic dignity of the individual – that is, human rights; and to advance fundamental social justice. But to do so,' he continues, 'not just as Jeremiah and Isaiah railing outside the walls of Jerusalem, but by being on the bus as individual Christians.'

He notes 'the number of people I run into in the world who are quite bright, quite ethically literate, and you say, well, the public political marketplace needs folks like you. And they say, "Oh no, I couldn't do that." And you say, why? "I couldn't cope with the criticism." Oh really? The Nazarene copped a bit of that! The prophets got off easy – apart from all of them. Jeremiah got thrown onto a dung heap. So getting people out of the pulpit and into praxis is part of it – although we still need people in the pulpit, to keep those in praxis in focus.'

What might be the role of a theological institution in all of this? 'Many universities,' says Rudd, 'might scoff at the idea of theology as a university discipline, simply because it is beyond reason and beyond empiricism, and ultimately untestable. I think people need to confront that for the stupidity that it represents. At universities, we study theology, we study philosophy, we study literature, we study art, we study design – much of which is unmeasurable, and ultimately subjective, but still deals with realities that can be perceived and experienced beyond reason and beyond empiricism. In Australia we all need to become more comfortable talking about spirituality – because it's a dimension of humanity – rather than pretending spirituality doesn't exist, or that it's inherently illegitimate, or a figment of my psychological imagination. We need to become comfortable with this, and not regard it as exotic.'

FURTHER READING

Kevin Rudd, *The Avoidable War: The Dangers of a Catastrophic Conflict Between the US and Xi Jinping's China*, Hachette Australia, 2022

Kevin Rudd, 'Scott Morrison's partisan interpretation of biblical passages is disturbing for democracy' in *The Guardian*, 1 May 2021

Kevin Rudd, *Kevin Rudd: The PM Years*, Pan Macmillan Australia, 2018

Kevin Rudd, *Not for the Faint-hearted: A Personal Reflection on Life, Politics and Purpose 1957-2007*, Pan Macmillan Australia, 2017

Conclusion

PETER SHERLOCK

WE BEGAN WRITING this book to explore a simple idea: that theology is not just for church. If theology matters – if it has any significance beyond particular faith communities – then theological ideas and practices should be evident in how we humans inform, shape and deepen our common life together. As this book took shape, we were struck by how eager people were to tell us about the ways in which theology had shaped their lives and work. In some cases, it seemed like they had just been waiting for someone to ask.

In Australia today, studying theology can seem like an odd choice. Much of our higher education system is geared towards 'job outcomes'. A previous government spoke explicitly about the need for more 'job-ready' graduates. There is an overwhelming emphasis on *what* you will do at the end of your studies, not *how* or *why* you will do it. Theology, on the other hand, is fundamentally about the 'how' and the 'why'. It teaches us to look at the world in a different light: to see the planet and other people as emerging from and deeply related to a mysterious but loving Creator, and to examine contemporary problems through the lens of an ancient message of peace, justice, grace and forgiveness. Theology is concerned with formation, with who we are and who we might become, and invites us to re-imagine ourselves not as individuals but as deeply connected by mutual responsibility, one for the other.

These themes and more emerged from the conversations we had for this book. So what have we learned along the way about why and how theology matters in contemporary and future Australia?

We need to be clear about what theology is and what it is for. On the one hand, the participants in this book demonstrate that theology is most definitely not only for the churches. On the other, it is not the 'queen of the sciences', an ultimate academic discipline that can solve all our problems. In asking questions about God, theology prompts us humans to think beyond ourselves and our immediate concerns, and to come to grips with our spiritual reality alongside other aspects of our being. Theology provides a set of texts, methodologies and premises – perhaps better, parables, stories and images – that help us ask big questions about where we are, who we are, and how we are called to live, including mysteries like love, suffering, joy and hope that we can never fully comprehend.

Guided by this understanding of theology, we can articulate five reasons why theological education is as important as ever in Australia today – why 'theology matters'.

The first is that the antidote to bad theology is not no theology at all but rather good theology. The effects of bad theology can be seen all around us: in the ongoing injustices experienced by First Peoples in Australia, for example, many of which have their historical roots in misreadings of Biblical texts. Bad theology is also behind the subjugation of women in certain churches which can validate and even encourage gender-based violence. It is behind the trauma experienced by many LGBTQIA+ people of faith who seek love and acceptance in church communities only to find the opposite. And it is behind the cover-ups of child sex abuse exposed by the Royal Commission – sometimes it is even behind the abuse itself. In a world where religion is playing more of a role, not less, to expunge theology from public life is simply not an option. Bad theology must be countered by better theology.

The second reason we need theology is that it offers critical apparatus to examine our values, beliefs and behaviours. This includes rigorous self-examination, the willingness to acknowledge error and failure, and steps towards the repentance and conversion necessary to fulfil our potential. Theology calls attention to the needs of others – love of God, love of neighbour – and what it might mean to live relationally, to act in the interests of the common good, to stand in solidarity with the marginalised. It's this drive to do things differently in a world obsessed with individual success that engenders the passion for justice, truth and ethics found in the stories told in this book.

The third reason theology matters is that our public discourse is not in a good way. In Australia and globally, much public speech lacks sound judgment and mutual compassion. We descend into culture wars at the drop of a hat. A healthy democratic political community needs strong and informed voices from every part of society, and forms of dialogue that are sustained, enduring and capable of supporting long-term change. Where theology is ignored the public conversation is impoverished. This makes it impossible, for example, to engage adequately with moral and spiritual questions such as how to respond to the First Peoples of this land. Aboriginal and Torres Strait Islanders live out of a deep and ancient Wisdom, and theology can help provide a language to acknowledge this and work towards mutual understanding.

The fourth reason theology matters is that we are all spiritual beings. A common complaint about our contemporary Australian lifestyle centres around a constellation of issues we might describe as 'busyness'. This includes the lack of work/life balance, the endless media cycle of instant news, the multiple technologies that invade our thoughts and bodies by day and by night, the increasing absence of any experience of simply thinking, reading, pondering. Theology expects us to spend time in discernment before rushing into action. Indeed, theology contains a rich store of values and practices that can challenge this culture of busyness. One such practice is contemplation, central to Christian tradition, a practice requiring the counter-cultural patience to wait, listen, observe instead of rushing headlong into action.

The fifth and final reason we need theology is that theology teaches us how to die – and therefore how to live. The ultimate truth all humans must confront is that we will all die. Until relatively recently, a critical theme of education, and of religion, was preparation for death. In medieval Europe, this was encapsulated in the arts of death, or *memento mori*, which taught people how to die well. A core purpose of the arts of death was, paradoxically, to teach us how to live in light of our mortality. In modern societies such as Australia, which enjoy tremendous wealth (notwithstanding the poverty of many of our citizens), theology is the only discipline left that can prepare us for our fate. A renewed purpose for theology in this present, confused and apocalyptic age is to encourage us to learn to live.

The lives of each of the people in this book have been shaped by their engagement with theology, and many were eager to share just how influential this has been. There are many more people across Australia we could have included, of course, and there are many people of other religious traditions who can tell similar stories. Australia is a multicultural country, which means Australia is a multi-faith country. This is a great gift to any nation. Humans across the world and across the centuries have sought and thought about the divine, however they understand the divine to be. We hope this book will provide a glimpse of what this kind of thinking can mean in Australian lives today.

A critical part of any theological endeavour, and perhaps especially theological education, must be humility. To engage with theology is to acknowledge there are forces, ideas and values greater than any of us, greater than our abilities, achievements or aspirations. True humility is not about what you do or what you say. It is a grace, a gift, a disposition, a way of life. True humility includes accepting the authority of the elders, being willing to place ourselves under the mighty hand of the Creator. These are truths our society would do well to observe, whatever our personal faith, by drawing on the living traditions of Christian wisdom and the cultural practices of Aboriginal and Torres Strait Islander societies, traditions that require attention to the wisdom of the elders. For in humble obedience lies great strength – I, you, can set aside the foolish pride that makes us think we have to solve all the problems, that only we can carry all the burdens. To be truly humble is to rejoice in our mutual dependence. True humility requires us first to recognise then to respond to our calling with confidence and self-awareness. True humility means exercising our authority with respect for each other and for the common good.

At this precarious moment in human history, each of us needs the humility, self-recognition, wisdom of the elders, and discipline of courage that theology can supply. War, pandemic, climate change, the decline of Christian faith in the west, the legacy of colonialism and slavery, the unjust discrimination within both church and society, the harm we cause to each other, the unravelling of democracy itself – these are tough times.

And so theology matters as much as it ever has. Theology teaches us to think outside the box. Theology makes us recognise the unspoken values and paradigms that underpin our behaviours. Theology requires the grace of humility to recognise there is a better way to live and a better way to die. Perhaps above all, theology can endow us with courage to turn ourselves and our world towards that brighter destination.

Almost every person we met in preparing this book spoke about hope. Hope is the ground of Christian theology, and it manifests itself in many ways. Doing theology at all in the face of great evil is itself a gesture, however feeble it might seem at the time, of hope. In 2023, Australia had a referendum to decide whether to acknowledge Indigenous Australians in the Constitution and give them a Voice to Parliament. The referendum failed badly. Many First Nations people were devastated. Many other Australians were devastated too. The day after the referendum, Anne Pattel-Gray appeared on the ABC news discussion program *The Drum*. At the end of the program she was asked if she had any final words.

'I say to my mob out there, our people,' she said after a pause. 'Take comfort that the ancestors are with you. That they give us strength to continue in our struggle. And that we take courage, and build on our resilience, to continue the fight for justice. Be with one another, and' – here she raised a hand – 'may the Creator be with you.'

It was a moment of grace; a glimpse, in a dark time, of hope.

And in the end, this is why theology matters.

Acknowledgments

PETER SHERLOCK and DANIEL NELLOR

WE EXPRESS OUR profound gratitude to each of the participants in this book – for agreeing to speak with us, for giving generously of their time and wisdom, and for being willing to put their stories before a larger audience.

Beyond our participants, several others supported us in producing this book through encouragement, conversation about our aims, or suggesting people we might approach. Thanks to Lisa Agaiby, Vicky Balabanski, Shenouda Boutros, Kerrie Burn, the late Austin Cooper OMI, John Flett, Wendy Mayer, Michael McGirr, Gabrielle McMullen, Janice McRandal, Chris Mulherin, Ben Myers, Paul Oslington, David Perry, and Robyn Whitaker.

Hugh McGinlay has made an inestimable contribution to Australian theology and spirituality as a publisher by providing a forum for scholarly and creative work to be read and disseminated for many decades. We are grateful for his enthusiasm for this book as with so many others.

Finally, we acknowledge the support of the University of Divinity, a unique and critically important institution for Australia. Peter is especially grateful for the University Council's encouragement to take time for research and writing, and to the staff, students and graduates of the University for theologically rich conversation and action across the last 12 years.

www.ingramcontent.com/pod-product-compliance
Lightning Source LLC
Chambersburg PA
CBHW012005090526
44590CB00026B/3883